Paris

DIRECTIONS

8ᵉ Arrᵗ

AVENUE

DES

CHAMPS-ÉLYSÉES

WRITTEN AND RESEARCHED BY

Ruth Blackmore and

James McConnachie

ROUGH GUIDES

NEW YORK • LONDON • DELHI

www.roughguides.com

Contents

4

INTRODUCTION

Introduction to

Paris

A trip to Paris, famous as the most romantic of destinations, is one of those lifetime musts. The very fabric of the city is elegant, its grand avenues and atmospheric little back-streets lined with harmonious apartment blocks and interspersed by exquisitely designed gardens and squares. The Parisians are no less stylish than their city: a sophisticated, cosmopolitan people renowned for their chic and their hauteur.

▶ The Seine from Pont des Arts

Through the heart of the city flows the Seine, skirting the pair of islands where Paris was founded. The historic pillars of the city, the church of Notre-Dame and the royal palace of the Louvre, stand on the riverbank, along with one of the world's most distinctive landmarks – the Eiffel Tower. There are legions of art galleries and museums

When to visit

Spring is the classic time to visit Paris, when the weather is mild (average daily 6–20°C), with bright days balanced by rain showers. **Autumn**, similarly mild, and **winter** (1–7°C) can be very rewarding, but on overcast days the city can feel melancholy; winter sun on the other hand is the city's most flattering light, and hotels and restaurants are relatively uncrowded in this season. By contrast, Paris in high **summer** (15–25°C) is not the best time to go: large numbers of Parisians desert the capital between July 15 and the end of August for the beach or mountains, and many restaurants and shops close down for much of this period.

▶ Secré-Couer, Montmartre

Alongside the great civic museums and monuments lie well-defined *quartiers* that make Paris feel more a collection of sophisticated villages than a true metropolis. Traditional communities still revolve around the local cafés, while wealthier enclaves preserve their exclusive boutiques and restaurants. Quarters such as the elegant Marais, chi-chi St-Germain and romantic Montmartre are ideal for shopping, sitting in cafés and just aimlessly wandering, while throughout the city you can find peaceful green spaces, ranging from formal gardens and avant-garde municipal parks to

too: between the Musée du Louvre, the Musée d'Orsay and the Pompidou Centre, you can see an unhealthy proportion of the world's finest works of art. For those willing to venture beyond the city limits, the glorious Gothic cathedral of St-Denis, the sumptuous royal palace of Versailles and the all-singing, all-dancing Disneyland Paris, are easily accessible.

▶ View from Tour Montparnasse

◄ Tuileries Gardens

ancient cemeteries.

Few cities can compete with the thousand-and-one cafés, brasseries and restaurants that dot Paris's boulevards and back-alleys, from ultra-modern fashion temples to traditional mir-rored palaces, and from tiny gourmet bistrots to crowded Vietnamese din-ers. After dark, the theatres and concert halls host world-leading productions, and tiny venues put on jazz gigs and Parisian *chanson* nights, while the café-bars and clubs of the Champs-Elysées, the Bastille and the Left Bank fill with the young and style-conscious from all over Europe, and beyond.

◄ Bastille Café

>> PARIS AT A GLANCE

▶ Notre-Dame

The Marais

One of Paris's most captivating districts, the Marais brims with trendy bars and cafés, not to mention gorgeous Renaissance mansions, some of which house outstanding museums.

The Islands

The Ile de la Cité's soaring Notre-Dame and glittering Sainte-Chapelle have been inspiring visitors for centuries, while picturesque Ile Saint-Louis is ideal for leisurely quai-side strolling.

▶ Beaubourg Metro

◀ Marais shopwindow

Champs Elysées

Synonymous with glitz and glamour, the Champs Elysées sweeps through one of the city's most exclusive districts, studded with luxury hotels and top fashion boutiques.

Beaubourg

At the heart of the ancient Beaubourg quartier stands the resolutely modern Pompidou Centre, its riot of coloured tubing concealing a matchless collection of modern art.

▲ Place du Tertre, Montmartre

▶Yves Saint Laurent, Left Bank

Left Bank

Paris's Left Bank, south of the Seine, is a real haven from the urban bustle of the city's Right-Bank core. The studenty Quartier Latin, fashionable St-Germain, arty Montparnasse and the elegant quarter around the Eiffel Tower all share a relaxed, village-like feel.

Montmartre

Hilltop views of the city, traffic-free streets, rich artistic associations and great cafés make Montmartre the most charming of Paris's neighbourhoods.

Eastern Paris

Traditionally the working-class area, eastern Paris's diverse stu-dent, arty and ethnic mix ensures a vibrant café and nightlife scene.

Ideas

The big six

The appeal of Paris very much lies in its ability to feel like two cities. One is a place of grand monuments and world-class museums; the other a surprisingly small-town kind of place, of low-rise apartments, local shops and neighbourhood cafés. You should save a little time to explore the more intimate side of the city, but the **landmark sights** certainly shouldn't be missed, especially if it's your first time in Paris – even if you've visited many times before, it would be hard to tire of the Sainte-Chapelle or Eiffel Tower, and you could spend days strolling around the Louvre alone.

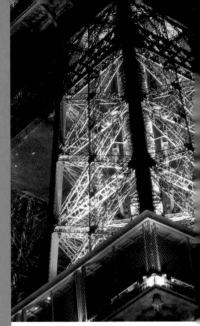

The Eiffel Tower

The closer you get, the more impressive the Eiffel Tower becomes. From the top, it's just magnificent.

▸P.136 ▸ THE EIFFEL TOWER AREA ▲

Sacré-Cœur

Crowning the Butte Montmartre, the white-domed Sacré-Cœur is an essential part of the city skyline.

▸P.155 ▸ MONTMARTRE ▲

The Louvre

The Louvre is simply one of the greatest art galleries in the world, with a palatial setting worthy of the collection inside.

▶P74 ▶ THE LOUVRE ▼

Pompidou Centre

Famous for its radical "inside-out" architecture, the Pompidou Centre is one of the city's most recognizable and popular landmarks.

▶P.99 ▶ BEAUBOURG AND LES HALLES ▼

Notre-Dame

The great Gothic cathedral of Notre-Dame, with its delicate tracery, exquisite rose windows and soaring nave, is an awe-inspiring sight.

▶P.70 ▶ THE ISLANDS ▲

Sainte-Chapelle

The sumptuous interior of the Sainte-Chapelle, its walls comprised almost entirely of stained glass ranks among the finest achievements of French High Gothic.

▶P.68 ▶ THE ISLANDS ▲

Paris calendar

Famously described by Hemingway as "a moveable feast", Paris won't disappoint whatever time of year you visit. You'll see another side to the city, however, if you time your trip to coincide with one of its key **festivals or events**. Turn up on **Bastille Day**, for example, and you'll find Parisians in carnival mood, celebrating the 1789 storming of the Bastille with fireworks and parties. Later on in July, you can join the crowds lining the Champs Elysées to cheer home the **Tour de France** and then work off the excitement by lying back in a deckchair on the Seine's **Paris Plage**.

Paris Plage

For four weeks in the height of summer, tonnes of sand are laid out as a beach along a stretch of the Seine, creating a kind of Paris-sur-Mer.

▶ P.206 ▶ ESSENTIALS ▲

Bastille Day

July 14 is the country's most important national holiday, celebrated with dancing, fireworks and a military parade down the Champs Elysées.

▶ P.206 ▶ ESSENTIALS ▲

The Tour de France

Join in with the excitement as the world's
most famous cycle race sprints home down
the Champs Elysées at the end of July.

▶ P.206 ▶ ESSENTIALS

Foire du Trône

One of the city's biggest funfairs, held in
April and May, in the Bois de Vincennes.

▶ P.206 ▶ ESSENTIALS

Nuit Blanche

During Nuit Blanche (Sleepless Night)
hundreds of galleries, cafés and public
buildings remain open all night, with music
and cultural events held city wide.

▶ P.206 ▶ ESSENTIALS

The Seine

Sometimes referred to as Paris's main avenue, the Seine sashays through the centre in a broad arc, dividing the Left Bank from the Right Bank and taking in the capital's grandest monuments on its way. It was the Seine that brought the city into being and for centuries was its lifeblood, a major conduit of trade and commerce. These days, its leafy **quais** provide welcome havens from the city's bustle and its numerous **bridges** afford fine and unexpected vistas, while **river trips** are a relaxing way to see some of the capital's best-known sights.

Bateaux Mouches

An hour's trip in a Bateau Mouche is a great way to get a close-up view of the classic buildings along the Seine.

▶ P.207 ▶ ESSENTIALS ▲

The quais

The tree-lined *quais* are perfect for relaxing walks or a restful pause, especially on Sundays when parts of the Right Bank *quai* are closed to traffic.

▶ P.116 ▶ QUARTIER LATIN ▲

Pont Alexandre III

The most extravagant bridge in the city –
witness its single iron arch spanning 109m,
topped off with exuberant Art Deco lamps
and statues of river nymphs.

▸ P.136 ▸ THE EIFFEL TOWER AREA ▼

Pont des Arts

The Pont des Arts is a graceful link between
the Louvre and St-Germain, with its
benches perfect for sitting out in the sunshine and gazing as the river flows by.

▸ P.128 ▸ ST-GERMAIN ▼

Pont-Neuf

Built in 1607, this elegant arched bridge is
Paris's oldest and affords fine downstream
views.

▸ P.68 ▸ THE ISLANDS ▲

Batobus

A refreshing and picturesque change to the
Métro, this handy river bus calls at many of
the big sights, including Notre-Dame and
the Louvre.

▸ P.204 ▸ ESSENTIALS ▲

Contemporary architecture

Over the past few decades Paris has commissioned some of the boldest **architectural projects** in Europe. A large number are the legacy of François Mitterrand, who, like many a leader of France before him, was keen to leave his stamp on the capital and enhance the nation's prestige. Many of his projects, such as the glass pyramid erected in the very heart of the Louvre palace, were hugely controversial at first but are now widely admired, testament to a new go-ahead spirit in the city.

Fondation Cartier

The Fondation Cartier's art gallery remains the most perfect expression of Jean Nouvel's work, its walls apparently dissipating into planes of glass and light-filled air.

▶ P.146 ▶ MONTPARNASSE ▼

Grande Arche de la Défense

The sheer scale of this contemporary riposte to the Arc de Triomphe is staggering.

▶ P.178 ▶ WESTERN PARIS ▼

Bibliothèque Nationale

Dominique Perrault's four book-shaped glass towers are an astounding sight, but it's the garden sunk between them that makes this one of Paris's boldest buildings.

▶ P.151 ▶ SOUTHERN PARIS ◀

Institut du Monde Arabe

Jean Nouvel's Arab institute is best loved for its exquisite *moucharabiyah* facade, which blends traditional Arabic art with the latest technology.

▶ P.117 ▶ QUARTIER LATIN ▼

Cité des Sciences

Four times the size of the Pompidou Centre, this stunningly huge complex is the science museum to end all science museums.

▶ P.170 ▶ EASTERN PARIS ▲

The Pyramid

I.M. Pei's glass pyramid arose in 1989 in the Louvre's historic courtyard, initially shocking all of Paris.

▶ P.74 ▶ THE LOUVRE ▼

Art galleries

Paris's **galleries** house one of the finest concentrations of art in the world, ranging from the vast treasure trove of the Louvre to small, specialist collections built up by wealthy individuals. The city's collections encompass Greek and Roman **antiquities**, oriental art and masterpieces representing all the major art movements from the Renaissance onwards. As well as exceptional paintings by **native artists** such as Matisse, Monet and Renoir, there is a particularly rich legacy of works by **foreign painters** – Kandinsky, Picasso and Dalí among them – who were drawn to the city in the nineteenth and early twentieth centuries a time when, for any aspiring artist, Paris was the only place to be.

Musée Marmottan

Monet's paintings of Giverny, as well as several of his *Waterlilies*, steal the show at this gallery of Impressionists.

▶ P.177 ▶ WESTERN PARIS ▲

The Louvre

The Louvre's collections represent not just the best of all French art, but also Egyptian, Greek, Roman and Islamic pieces, as well as superb galleries of European painting and sculpture.

▶ P.74 ▶ THE LOUVRE ▲

Musée Picasso

The largest collection of Picassos any-where, displayed in a beautiful Renaissance mansion.

▸P.108 ▸ THE MARAIS

Site de Création Contemporaine

A cutting edge gallery and exhibition space, this fills the contemporary art gap in the great national collections.

▸P.88 ▸ TROCADERO ▸

Musée National d'Art Moderne, Pompidou Centre

One of the finest collections of modern art in the world, with major holdings of works by Kandinsky, Picasso and Matisse.

▸P.100 ▸ BEAUBOURG AND LES HALLES ▾

Musée d'Orsay

This converted railway station provides a cathedral-like setting for the greatest works of French Impressionism.

▸P.132 ▸ ST-GERMAIN ▴

Lesser-known museums

Paris boasts a host of **lesser-known** but first-rate **museums**, often overlooked by visitors, and consequently much less crowded than, say, the Louvre or the Orsay. You can explore subjects as diverse as the history of Judaism in France, eighteenth-century decorative arts, and the history of the city's sewers (*les égouts*), as well as viewing some fascinating artefacts, ranging from Khmer sculpture at the Musée Guimet to Neolithic dug-out canoes at the Musée Carnavalet. Many museums, moreover, enjoy beautiful settings, such as fine Renaissance mansions, showing off their collections to full advantage.

Musée d'Art et d'Histoire du Judaïsme

You could easily spend a couple of hours and not notice the time passing in this absorbing museum devoted to the history and art of Jews in Europe and North Africa.

▸ P.105 ▸ THE MARAIS ▲

Musée Carnavalet

A fascinating museum that brings the history of Paris alive through a wealth of paintings and artefacts and some wonderful old interiors, rescued from houses pulled down to make way for Haussmann's redevelopments.

▸ P.109 ▸ THE MARAIS ▼

Musée d'Art Moderne de la Ville de Paris

The city's own art collection specializes in paintings of or about Paris itself, making this one of the most rewarding and intimate of the larger art galleries.

▸ P.88 ▸ TROCADERO ▲

Musée Guimet

Visiting the beautifully designed Musée Guimet, with its refined statues and sculptures from all over the Buddhist world, is a distinctly spiritual experience.

▸ P.07 ▸ TROCADERO ▼

Musée Cognacq-Jay

A small but choice collection of eighteenth-century paintings and decorative art built up by a family of philanthropists and art lovers, the Cognacq-Jays.

▸ P.109 ▸ THE MARAIS ▲

House museums

To summon up the ghosts of the city's past, you could take in paintings of Parisian scenes like Renoir's *Bal du Moulin de la Galette*, in the Musée d'Orsay, or read great Parisian novels like Hugo's *Les Misérables* or Maupassant's *Bel Ami*, but you'd do as well to visit one of the city's **historic houses**. Many have been turned into museums and the best preserve an original **writer's study or artist's studio**. Seeing intimate domestic details like a stove, bed or sideboard, or admiring the cool north light through high studio windows, is an excellent antidote to the grander scale of the city outside.

Musée Rodin

Rodin's elegant studio home now houses the definitive collection of the sculptor's powerful, mould-breaking works.

▶P.140 ▶ EIFFEL TOWER AREA ▼

Musée Jacquemart-André

This sumptuous Second Empire residence, built for the art-loving Jacquemart-André couple, displays their choice collection of Italian, Dutch and French masters.

▶P.82 ▶ THE CHAMPS-ELYSEES AND TUILERIES ▼

Maison de Balzac

The house lived in by Balzac in the 1840s preserves the simple desk where he would write for up to eighteen hours at a time for weeks on end.

▶ P.177 ▶ WESTERN PARIS ▲

Musée Moreau

Gustave Moreau's eccentric canvases cover every inch of his spacious studio's walls; immediately below, you can visit the tiny apartment where the artist lived with his parents.

▶ P.159 ▶ MONTMARTRE AND
NORTHERN PARIS ▲

Musée Bourdelle

The heroic scale of Bourdelle's proto-Modernist sculptures is perfectly balanced by the homely, just-as-he-left-it feel of the sculptor's studio and living quarters.

▶ P.144 ▶ MONTPARNASSE ▼

Musée Delacroix

Delacroix lived and worked in this pretty studio building, where you can see some of his smaller works as well as some personal effects.

▶ P.129 ▶ ST-GERMAIN ▼

Walks and gardens

Of all the ways to get under the skin of Paris, perhaps the most satisfying is just to appreciate the peace in one of the city's harder-to-find **little gardens**, or take a **short walk** along the elegant promenades that can be found here and there, with a bit of looking. Quite apart from their charm, and the pleasure to be found in discovering them, these hidden nooks and quiet breathing spaces are wonderful for people-watching: this is where you'll find Parisians walking their dogs, playing with their kids, reading, hand-holding, and just taking time out from the city.

Promenade Plantée

Get a different angle on the city from this old railway viaduct, now an elevated walkway planted with a glorious abundance of trees and flowers.

▶ P.164 ▶ THE BASTILLE ▲

Jardin Atlantique

Although a public park, the Jardin Atlantique is actually hidden away on top of the Montparnasse railway tracks – a triumph of engineering and contemporary garden design.

▶ P.142 ▶ MONTPARNASSE ▲

Place Dauphine

Relax and watch a spot of leisurely *boules* being played under the chestnuts of this peaceful and secluded square.

▶ P.68 ▶ THE ISLANDS ▼

Jardin du Palais Royal

Enclosed by a stately ensemble of arcaded buildings and little frequented, the Jardin du Palais Royal feels like a secret garden in the middle of the city.

▶ P.94 ▶ THE GRANDS BOULEVARDS ▲
AND PASSAGES

Canal St-Martin

With its elegant arched bridges and leafy *quais*, the Canal St-Martin is a charming spot for a stroll.

▶ P168 ▶ EASTERN PARIS ▶

Allée des Cygnes

One of the most unusual Paris walks, this takes you along a tree-lined embankment adrift in the Seine and proffers dramatic views of the post-industrial western riverbanks.

▶ P.150 ▶ SOUTHERN PARIS ▼

Dead Paris

From the royal tombs at St-Denis to the memorials at the Panthéon and Napoleon's tomb at Les Invalides, the **dead of Paris** certainly make their presence felt. It's the cemeteries, however, that make the biggest impact on the city's landscape. From vantage points like the Eiffel Tower they seem to fill a surprising amount of the city's area, looking like green islands speckled with miniature stone apartment blocks. Père-Lachaise is a major draw, but don't miss the smaller graveyards at Montmartre and Montparnasse. The most morbid sight of all, the bone-lined catacombs, is covered in "Underground Paris" (see p.146).

Père-Lachaise cemetery

Pay homage to Chopin, Oscar Wilde or Jim Morrison – just some of the countless notables buried in what is arguably the world's most famous cemetery.

▶ P.171 ▶ EASTERN PARIS

Montparnasse cemetery

You can seek out the graves of Baudelaire, Beckett, Sartre and de Beauvoir at Montparnasse cemetery, and admire the powerful Brancusi sculpture of *The Kiss*.

▶ P.145 ▶ MONTPARNASSE

Napoleon's tomb

The emperor's magnificently pompous tomb is the highlight of the great military complex of Les Invalides.

P.139 ▸ THE EIFFEL TOWER AREA ▲

Panthéon

Moving their remains to the crypt of the Panthéon is the greatest honour the French Republic can bestow on its artists, poets, thinkers and politicians.

P.120 ▸ QUARTIER LATIN ◀

Montmartre cemetery

Zola's grave, its effigy often graced by a rose, is found at Montmartre, along with other artistic greats Stendhal, Degas and François Truffaut.

P.157 ▸ MONTMARTRE AND NORTHERN PARIS ▼

Gastronomic restaurants

Paris boasts an unparalleled concentration of **haute-cuisine restaurants** and is the perfect place to blow out on the meal of a lifetime. Not only will the food be some of the most sublime you've ever tasted but the service will be impeccable – attentive yet discreet . Also, while the decor might be *belle époque* or Louis XV, gastronomic cuisine doesn't have to mean astronomic prices, some restaurants offer a **set lunch menu** for around €60. In the evening prices average at €150 for three courses, and there's no limit on the amount you can pay for fine wines.

L'Ambroisie

Beautiful tapestries provide a fitting backdrop to this intimate and refined restaurant, which serves exquisite and creative cuisine.

▶ P.114 ▶ THE MARAIS ▲

Taillevent

Michelin three-star rated since 1973 – no mean achievement – *Taillevent* won't fail to please with its ever-inventive dishes and outstanding wine cellar.

▶ P.85 ▶ THE CHAMPS-ELYSEES ▲
AND TUILERIES

Lasserre

A classic haute-cuisine establishment with a lovely *belle époque* dining room and a roof that is rolled back to reveal the Paris sky on balmy summer evenings.

▶P.84 ▶ **THE CHAMPS-ELYSEES AND TUILERIES** ▶

Jules Verne

It's hard to decide which is better at Jules Verne, the view from the second floor of the Eiffel Tower or the truly excellent contemporary French cuisine. You'll need to book a few months in advance and dress your best for the trip up the private lift.

▶P.141 ▶ **EIFFEL TOWER AREA** ▼

Alain Ducasse at the Plaza Athénée

One of the most innovative chefs around, Alain Ducasse sends diners into raptures over his exquisite food and ultra-stylish decor – Louis XV chandeliers draped with shimmering, metallic organza

▶P.84 ▶ **THE CHAMPS-ELYSEES AND TUILERIES** ▲

Great Parisian restaurants

One of the chief pleasures of a visit to Paris is deciding where to eat – not least because the choice is so good. While the city is justly famed for its haute-cuisine restaurants, there is no shortage of places where you can eat extremely well for a modest outlay. The Marais Quartier Latin, and Saint-Germain are particularly well supplied with excellent places, but nearly every *quartier* has its local that serves food to very high standards. We've selected just a few of our favourite haunts below, chosen for their cuisine, ambience and decor.

Chartier

Opened in 1896 to serve affordable meals to thousands of Auvergnats fleeing poverty and hardship in the Massif Central, *Chartier* is still going strong, its decor little changed and its food as cheap and good value as ever.

▶ P.97 ▶   THE GRANDS BOULEVARDS ▼

Le Reminet

This small, relaxed restaurant has a really enjoyable mixture of inventive style and friendly homeliness, both in its cuisine and its ambience.

▶ P127 ▶   QUARTIER LATIN ▼

Au Bourguignon du Marais

A little outpost of Burgundy, serving up delicious regional specialities, paired with carefully chosen wines.

▸ **P.114** ▸ **THE MARAIS** ▼

L'Avant Goût

Hidden away near the Butte-aux-Cailles, this tiny restaurant is in the vanguard of *bistrot* cuisine: fresh, exciting flavours cooked with panache and served without excessive fuss.

▸ **P.151** ▸ **SOUTHERN PARIS** ▼

A la Pomponette

Deeply old-fashioned and in the heart of Montmartre, the *Pomponette* is already halfway to being a classic bistrot. Add traditional, lovingly prepared cuisine and you've got a winner.

▸ **P.160** ▸ **MONTMARTRE AND NORTHERN PARIS** ▲

Pitchi Poï

The warmth of *Pitchi Poï*'s flavoured Polish vodkas is more than matched by the convivial surroundings and friendly service at this fine Jewish/central European restaurant.

▸ **P.115** ▸ **THE MARAIS** ▲

Classic brasseries

First brought to Paris by immigrant Alsatians in the late nineteenth century, **brasseries** were originally simple beer taverns ("brasserie" means "brewery"). Over the years, they have added full dinner menus and continue to offer an authentic taste of Parisian life with many preserving their fine *belle époque* interiors – globe lamps, glass cupolas, brass fittings and dark-leather banquettes. They're delightfully bustling places: white-aproned waiters dash up and down bearing enormous platters of seafood, steak or sauerkraut – and you'll find them just as animated late into the night as they are in the early evening, full of the post-theatre and concert crowd taking advantage of the late opening hours.

Bofinger

Bastille opera-goers pack the tables beneath this classic brasserie's splendid glass cupola.

▸P.167 ▸ THE BASTILLE ▲

Lipp

Lipp is a St-Germain classic: the haunt of powerful editors and media faces, it serves wonderful sauerkraut, among other traditional brasserie *plats*.

▸P.135 ▸ ST-GERMAIN ▲

Le Vaudeville

This lively establishment, attractively decorated with marble and mosaics, serves gigantic seafood platters and is especially popular with the post-theatre crowd.

▸ P.97 ▸ THE GRANDS BOULEVARDS AND PASSAGES ▼

La Coupole

You can recapture something of the spirit of Montparnasse's fashionable heyday at this giant, high-ceilinged brasserie, packed with drinkers and diners into the small hours.

▸ P.147 ▸ MONTPARNASSE ▼

Flo

This deeply old-fashioned brasserie is hidden away in an atmospheric courtyard near the Porte St-Denis in northern Paris, but it's well worth the journey.

▸ P.161 ▸ MONTMARTRE AND NORTHERN PARIS ▲

Le Square Trousseau

Set on an attractive square, this handsome brasserie attracts a chic but relaxed clientele.

▸ P.167 ▸ THE BASTILLE ▲

Cafés

Chilling out in **cafés** is one of the chief pleasures of a trip to Paris and the best way to get your finger on the city's pulse. A mainstay of Parisian society, cafés are places where people come to pose and people-watch, debate and discuss or simply read a book, knowing that once they've bought their drink, the waiter will leave them undisturbed for hours at a time. Some places have a chameleon-like existence, changing from quiet places for coffee in the daytime to buzzing venues – more like bars – in the evening. Whether you prefer Left Bank literary haunts or hip, stylish joints in the Marais and Bastille, you're bound to find somewhere that appeals.

Bar du Marché

The "market bar" pulls in the punters from St-Germain's busy old market street, rue de Buci, adding a dash of fashion-conscious, youthful style to the area.

▸P.134▸ ST-GERMAIN

Café de l'Industrie

One of Bastille's best cafés – young and busy yet comfortable and unpretentious – this is the kind of place that's hard to leave once you're ensconced.

▸P.166▸ THE BASTILLE

Café de la Mosquée

The café at the Paris mosque offers a taste of North Africa right in the heart of the Quartier Latin. Try the mint tea and delicious pastries.

▸P.124 ▸ QUARTIER LATIN ▼

L'Apparemment Café

A chic but comfortable café, with a warren of cosy back rooms that makes it good for unwinding in; you can play board games, too.

▸P.113 ▸ THE MARAIS ▲

Le Petit Fer à Cheval

A very attractive small café with a marble-topped bar in the shape of a horseshoe (fer à cheval), ideal for an aperitif or pick-me-up espresso.

▸P.114 ▸ THE MARAIS ▶

Café Charbon

An attractively revamped early twentieth-century café, attracting a young, trendy crowd.

▸P.173 ▸ EASTERN PARIS ▼

Paris nightlife

Many of Paris's best **café-bars** stay open very late, so after midnight you're not necessarily committed to a full-on **club**. If you do go clubbing, you'll find most Parisian DJs playing house or techno, but the musical style and general vibe really depends on who's running the individual *soirée*. Check out gay and lesbian venues too (see p.48), many of which attract trendy, mixed crowds. Taxis are hard to find after hours, so Parisian clubbers often keep going until after 5.30am, when the Métro restarts, or stay up even later at a fashionable "after" event.

Pause Café
What starts as a laid-back café in the daytime becomes a busy, trendy nightspot after midnight, with pavement tables, relaxed music and lots of chatter.

▶ P.166 ▶ THE BASTILLE   ▲

Batofar
The boats moored beside the Bibliothèque Nationale host some of Paris's liveliest and least pretentious nightlife venues, and this former light-house ship is the coolest of the lot.

▶ P.152 ▶ SOUTHERN PARIS   ▲

La Folie en Tête

The Butte-aux-Cailles, down in southern
Paris, is renowned for its alternative, left-
wing spirit, and *La Folie en Tête* is the most
characterful of its friendly, laid-back bars.

▸P.151 ▸ SOUTHERN PARIS ▼

Bastille bars

The Bastille area is the liveliest place in
Paris for nightlife, with excellent venues
ranging from trendy, late-opening little
cafés to club-bars with DJs.

▸P.166 ▸ THE BASTILLE ▼

Les Bains

This flashy venue – once a bathhouse – has
been taken over by a cool set, so you'd better look beautiful to get past the bouncers.

▸P.104 ▸ BEAUBOURG AND LES HALLES ▲

Rex Club

For music, the *Rex* is one of the best, with
an excellent sound system, lots of space and
enough clout to pull in the top promoters.

▸P.98 ▸ THE GRAND BOULEVARDS
        AND PASSAGES ▼

Musical Paris

Paris has a stimulating and diverse musical scene as rich as in any leading capital city. Classical music, from the traditional to the cutting-edge, flourishes, while opera-lovers can choose between the glittering Opéra Garnier and the modern Opéra Bastille (see p.167). World music, too, has a strong following, with France's past links to North and West Africa meaning you're as likely to find the leading stars of Mali and Algeria living and performing in Paris as in their own countries. In the city's bars and clubs, techno and house tend to rule, while that most French of musical traditions, the *chanson*, has recently made a comeback and can be heard in select, intimate venues around the city.

Café de la Danse
An intimate and attractive club hosting rock, pop, world and folk music.

▶ P.167 ▶ THE BASTILLE ▲

Opéra Garnier
A more opulent setting for grand opera and ballet would be hard to imagine.

▶ P.92 ▶ THE GRANDS BOULEVARDS ▲
AND PASSAGES

New Morning

A cavernous space with spartan decor and often standing room only, but the jazz aficionados who flock here nightly to hear the big names on the circuit don't seem to mind.

▶P.161 ▶ MONTMARTRE AND
NORTHERN PARIS   ▲

Théâtre des Champs-Elysées

The premiere of Stravinsky's *Rite of Spring* caused a riot here in 1913; these days its varied programme of classical music, opera and dance is more likely to meet with hearty applause.

▶P.85 ▶ THE CHAMPS-ELYSEES
AND TUILERIES   ▼

Au Limonaire

This tiny dinner and *chanson* venue could hardly be more Parisian, showcasing up-and-coming talent in the best jazzy, comic-romantic-philosophical French tradition.

▶P.98 ▶ THE GRANDS BOULEVARDS ▲
AND PASSAGES

Gourmet Paris

You don't have to dine out to experience the **best of French food** in Paris. Supermarkets may have driven out some of the everyday grocers' and butchers' shops, but at the top end of the market you'll find plenty of deluxe *pâtisseries, chocolatiers, charcuteries, fromageries, traîteurs* and *épiceries*. Some are grand-scale, luxury food emporia, others bijou specialists where you can buy what the owner swears is the very best chocolate truffle, pâté or goat's cheese in the world. You'll also get the best advice on how to buy, keep, serve and ultimately eat your chosen treat, and it'll be meticulously well wrapped.

Mariage Frères

Caddies of familiar and exotic teas pack this delightful shop from floor to ceiling.

▸P.112 ▸ THE MARAIS ▲

Hédiard

Superlative-quality groceries, with sales staff as deferential as servants, as long as you don't try to reach for items yourself.

▸P.96 ▸ THE GRANDS BOULEVARDS ▲
AND PASSAGES

Barthélémy

The old shop front dates back to the days
when *Bartélémy* was a dairy. Now it sells
the best French cheeses.

▶P.133 ▶ ST-GERMAIN ▲

Debauve & Gallais

A temple to chocolate in the heart of St-
Germain. Endless inventive varieties are
made, displayed and finally wrapped up with
serious devotion to the art.

▶P.133 ▶ ST-GERMAIN ▼

Au Bon Marché

The food hall at the Bon Marché department
store is *the* place for fine French foods, as
well as luxury deli goods from around the
world.

▶P.133 ▶ ST-GERMAIN ▲

Fauchon

If there's a luxury French delicacy this food
emporium doesn't stock, then it isn't worth
knowing about.

▶P.96 ▶ THE GRANDS BOULEVARDS
AND PASSAGES ▼

Shops and markets

Some of the best places to shop in Paris have unusual venues. Two enormous **flea markets** squat just beyond the *périphérique* ring road, at the northern and southern fringes of the city, and you can pick up wonderful bargains and bric-a-brac at both, as well as much more upscale furnishings and curiosities. By contrast, you won't find many souvenirs at St-Denis' **suburban market**, but you will get a powerful flavour of the vibrant, ethnically mixed city that lies "beyond the walls". Back in the centre, the handsome, nineteenth-century **passages** house lots of fascinating **boutiques**, while the funky **shops** under the arches of the Viaduc des Arts specialize in design.

The Viaduc des Arts

The arches of this former railway viaduct now house over fifty workshops, including fashion and jewellery designers, violin-makers and tapestry restorers.

▶ P.165 ▶ THE BASTILLE ▲

The passages

Paris's nineteenth-century arcades are gradually being restored to their former glory and are excellent hunting grounds for unusual gifts and one-off buys.

▶ P.95 ▶ THE GRANDS BOULEVARDS AND PASSAGES ▼

St-Denis market

The market at suburban St-Denis is more than a little rough at the edges, but it's lively, funky and quite different from anything else you'll experience in Paris.

▶P.183 ▶ EXCURSIONS ▼

Puces de St-Ouen

A giant antiques emporium with an equally massive cheap clothing, jumble and grey-import market hanging onto its coat-tails, St-Ouen is the king of Paris's flea markets.

▶P157 ▶ MONTMARTRE AND NORTHERN PARIS ▼

Puces de Vanves

The Puces de Vanves is the most faithful to Paris's flea-market traditions, with stall after stall of curiosities, bric-a-brac and antique junk.

▶P.149 ▶ SOUTHERN PARIS ▲

Paris hotels

Paris may have some seriously **luxurious hotels**, such as the *Hôtel Bristol*, with its Gobelins tapestries and colonnaded gardens, but you don't have to pay over the odds for somewhere with character and atmosphere. The Marais and Left Bank yield many **moderately priced hotels** in converted old town houses, which often retain attractive original features such as stone walls and exposed beams. You can also find the odd gem right at the budget end of the scale: the *Henri IV*, run by the same family for generations, enjoys an unbeatable location on one of the most attractive squares at the heart of the city.

L'Hôtel

Famously, Oscar Wilde died in this hotel, and it has been restored with more than a touch of camp decadence, as well as serious luxury.

▶P.194 ▶ ACCOMMODATION   ▼

Hôtel Chopin

A charming, quiet hotel tucked away down an elegant nineteenth-century *passage*.

▶P.193 ▶ ACCOMMODATION   ▼

Hôtel du Globe

Friendly, well-located in the middle of St-Germain, and charmingly decorated in an eccentrically medieval style, the Globe has earned its reputation as a classic.

▶P.194 ▶ ACCOMMODATION   ▼

Hôtel Henri IV

Some of the rooms are very worn, but a number have recently been refurbished, and you can't beat the location on beautiful place Dauphine.

▶ P.189 ▶ ACCOMMODATION ▼

Hôtel Ermitage

If you're looking for a quiet, old-fashioned, romantic retreat, look no further than the *Ermitage*, hidden away on the eastern heights of Montmartre.

▶ P.196 ▶ ACCOMMODATION ▼

Hôtel Caron de Beaumarchais

A beautiful hotel decorated throughout in Louis XVI style, down to the pianoforte in reception.

▶ P.193 ▶ ACCOMMODATION ▲

Paris fashion

Paris remains the capital of **world fashion** - even if you agree with Yves St-Laurent that Paris Fashion Week is "a ridiculous spectacle better suited to a concert stage". If you're in the market for haute couture, or are enough of a fashion devotee to visit the exquisite, historic clothes on display at the Musée de la Mode, you'll find the shopping superb. Glitzy couture names and international ready-to-wear brands are thick on the ground in the Champs-Elysées and St-Germain quarters, while for independent little boutiques, scour the Marais and Bastille, or the area around Abbesses métro, near Montmartre.

Abbesses boutiques

Shoppers with an original frame of mind should make for the little streets around place des Abbesses, where there's a cluster of independent designers and boutiques for smaller women.

▶ P.155 ▶ MONTMARTRE AND NORTHERN PARIS

Isabel Marant

Isabel Marant may be young but she's a fully-fledged designer with a fast-growing reputation. Yet the prices of her exciting, sometimes showy ready-to-wear collections aren't stratospheric.

▸P.166 ▸ THE BASTILLE ▾

Musée de la Mode

If you can't wear the best, you can at least stare at it at the Fashion Museum, which holds fascinating exhibitions on exquisite and historic designer wear.

▸P.87 ▸ TROCADERO ▴

Zadig & Voltaire

If the budget doesn't stretch to couture you can find beautifully cut, original and flattering designs at this Paris-based chain, which has branches all over the city.

▸P.103 ▸ BEAUBOURG AND LES HALLES ▴

Le Mouton à Cinq Pattes

You can find rack upon rack of what the French call *stock* – back-catalogue, end-of-lino factory seconds – at this mini-chain of bargain clothes stores.

▸P.133 ▸ ST-GERMAIN ▾

Gay Paris

Paris isn't just **gay- and lesbian- friendly**, it positively revels in an atmosphere of openness, especially in the "pink triangle" around rue Ste-Croix de la Bretonnerie, in the heart of the fashionable Marais district. Even the city's mayor, Bertrand Delanoë, is openly gay. An excellent monthly magazine, *Têtu* ("Headstrong"), lists the best bars and clubs, and there's an ever-growing number of gay-oriented hotels and restaurants too. The scene's confidence and stylishness often spills over into straight nightlife: gay clubs such as *Pulp* attract a seriously cool straight clientele.

Le Mixer

Just a tiny little bar but a very lively one, with a DJ mixing it up from a pulpit-like platform, lots of stylish lighting and a friendly, gay/lesbian/bi/straight crowd.

▶P.114 ▶ THE MARAIS ▲

Le Pulp

There's something very different about this lesbian-run, mostly mixed club. It's friendlier, more laid-back and yet trendier than many others in Paris – and it plays the best music.

▶P.98 ▶ THE GRANDS BOULEVARDS AND PASSAGES ▼

Gay Pride

The big event of the calendar is the half-million-strong pride march on the last Saturday of June, with lots of spin-off concerts, parties and events.

▸P.206 ▸ ESSENTIALS ▲

Amnésia Café

The most relaxed and upmarket gay venue in the city, affecting a cosy, sofa-filled *Friends* vibe by day and lots of cocktail fuelled bonhomie at night.

▸P113 ▸ THE MARAIS ▶

L'Open Café

The original out-and-proud café, at the very apex of the "pink triangle". Famous for its tables outside on the street, which make a great venue for posing and people-watching.

▸P.113 ▸ THE MARAIS ▼

Kids Paris

The obvious lure of Disneyland aside, Paris has plenty of attractions and **activities** to keep most children happy: puppet shows, funfairs, zoos and adventure parks, not to mention more **off-beat attractions** such as the creepy catacombs (see p.146) and dingy sewers (see p.138). In addition, nearly every park, big or small, has its play area with swings and slides. Just as much of a delight for many children is Paris's vibrant **atmosphere**, with its street performers and buskers, lively pavement cafés and brightly lit carrousels.

Disneyland

Disney's vast theme park may not be very French but the children will love it. Even cynical adults may find it hard to resist the more exciting rides.

▶ P.184 ▶ EXCURSIONS ▲

Jardin d'Acclimatation

No child could fail to be enchanted by this wonderland of mini-canal and train rides, adventure parks, trampolines, bumper cars, puppet theatres and farm animals.

▶ P.178 ▶ WESTERN PARIS ▲

Parc de la Villette

The Géode Omnimax cinema is just one of the many attractions for kids in this futuristic park.

▶P.168 ▶ EASTERN PARIS ▼

Jardin du Luxembourg boats

One of the timeless pleasures of the Luxembourg gardens is hiring a toy boat and sailing it to and fro across the circular pond.

▶P.128 ▶ ST-GERMAIN ▲

Sandpits

Paris seems to have sandpits in spades – at least one in every park and recreation area, as in the Palais Royal garden here.

▶P.94 ▶ THE GRANDS BOULEVARDS AND PASSAGES ▼

Ethnic Paris

For all that Paris is one of the world's great **ethnically mixed cities,** you could be forgiven for not noticing, as the majority of the black and North African population lives out in the suburbs. The vigorously revived Jewish quarter, on the other hand, is right in the heart of the city. As a visitor, the best way to get a flavour of ethnic Paris is to try the food: Vietnamese and African cuisine is particularly well represented, alongside the famous couscous cafés. Alternatively, visit the wonderful Institut du Monde Arabe (see p.117) or try a hammam steam bath – an outing that has become a Parisian institution.

Vietnamese restaurants

The best restaurants in so-called Chinatown, in the south of Paris, are the Vietnamese ones. Try the pho soup and the excellent desserts.

▶P.150 ▶ SOUTHERN PARIS   ▲

Couscous

Couscous is North Africa's gift to Paris. You can find it everywhere, from fast-food cafés with just a couple of seats to more elaborate settings, such as the fine *belle époque Chez Omar* in the Marais.

▶P.115 ▶ **THE MARAIS**   ▲

Hammam at the Paris mosque

Of all Paris's hammams, or bath houses, the Paris mosque's feels the most authentic, and you can relax with a mint tea in the courtyard afterwards.

▶P.122 ▶ **QUARTIER LATIN**   ▲

The Jewish Quarter

Paris's lively Jewish quarter is little more than one street but there's no mistaking when you hit it, crammed full as it is of kosher food shops, Hebrew bookstores and falafel stalls.

▶P.110 ▶ **THE MARAIS**   ▲

Waly Fay

This cosy but elegant West African restaurant is distinctly upmarket. The stews are richly spiced and the ambience warm and welcoming.

▶P.174 ▶ **EASTERN PARIS**   ▼

Green Paris

Paris may lack the large open spaces of London or New York, but this is more than made up for by its **beautiful parks**, from the majestic formal gardens of the Tuileries and Jardin du Luxembourg to the wilder, less ordered green spaces of the Bois de Boulogne and Bois de Vincennes on the city's periphery. Paris's parks are places where people come to meet each other, relax and have fun: families stroll or sit out in the open-air cafés, elderly men play chess under the chestnut trees and children mess around in sandpits or get treated to pony rides.

Place des Vosges

The place des Vosges's harmonious ensemble of pink-brick buildings form an elegant backdrop to the attractive and popular garden at its centre.

▶P.111 ▶ THE MARAIS ▼

Bois de Boulogne

This huge swathe of parkland, with its many attractions, such as the Parc de Bagatelle rose garden, is a favourite Parisian retreat.

▶P.177 ▶ WESTERN PARIS ▼

Parc André-Citroën

On the edge of the city, sloping down to the river, this public park is famous for its imaginative design, balloon ride and its capricious, computer-controlled fountains.

▸P.148 ▸ SOUTHERN PARIS ▼

Jardin des Tuileries

The French formal garden par excellence: sweeping vistas, symmetrical flowerbeds and straight avenues.

▸P.82 ▸ THE CHAMPS-ELYSEES AND TUILERIES ▲

Jardin du Luxembourg

For all its splendid Classical design, the Luxembourg is still the most relaxed and friendly of Paris's parks.

▸P.128 ▸ QUARTIER LATIN ▼

Underground Paris

Paris presents a glamorous, unruffled facade to the world. Its monuments are beautifully kept, its boulevards regularly planned and its apartment blocks designed to an elegant, uniform standard. The best way to scratch that glossy surface is to **go underground**. You can walk through the **sewers** and the bone-lined **catacombs**, explore the foundations of the city's greatest religious monument, and of course you can travel on the Métro system. The rubber-wheeled ride may be soft and the service dependable but this isn't smooth, insulated travel. Down here you're rubbing shoulder to shoulder with real, working Paris.

The Catacombs

The fascinating, tunnel-like quarries underneath Montparnasse are lined with literally millions of human bones, evacuated from the overcrowded Paris cemeteries in the nineteenth century.

▶ P.146 ▶ MONTPARNASSE ▲

Crypte archéologique

This atmospheric site beneath the square of Notre-Dame reveals remains of medieval and Gallo-Roman houses, as well as the old cathedral.

▸P.71 ▸ THE ISLANDS ▾

Sewers

A fascinating underground exhibition on a little-known, but vital side of the city's life.

▸P.138 ▸ EIFFEL TOWER AREA ▴

The Métro

There's no better way to get around the city than by the fast and efficient Métro. The stations are stylish too.

▸P.203 ▸ ESSENTIALS ▾

Artistic and literary Paris

Generations of writers and artists from all over Europe and the Americas have made their home in Paris, for a time at least, and quarters such as Montmartre, Montparnasse and St-Germain are incredibly evocative of particular artistic eras. For the visitor, there's a peculiar thrill about warming the same café seat as Picasso or Hemingway; though today's prices mean you're more likely to be sitting next to a successful publisher than a penniless novelist. For the latter, you'll have to go to the classic Left Bank bookshop, Shakespeare & Co, where the staff all seem to be looking for Parisian inspiration.

Musée du Montparnasse

Montparnasse was *the* artistic Bohemia of the early twentieth century, and the Musée de Montparnasse holds excellent exhibitions of the era's great artists.

▶ P.144 ▶ MONTPARNASSE ▼

Shakespeare & Co

The original Shakespeare & Co that published Joyce's *Ulysses* was over on rue de l'Odéon, but this is still a superb English-language bookshop and literary meeting place.

▶ P.124 ▶ QUARTIER LATIN ▼

Le Select

Unlike its rivals, *Le Select* hasn't gone down the oysters-and-champagne route, and it preserves a strong flavour of the arty pre-war years, if not the prices.

▸P.147 ▸ MONTPARNASSE ▲

Montmartre

Before Montparnasse there was Montmartre, and this most romantic of quarters still attracts visitors eager to see the streets and squares made famous by Picasso, Toulouse-Lautrec and others.

▸P.153 ▸ MONTMARTRE AND ▲
NORTHERN PARIS

Café Flore

The classic existentialist haunt is now more fashion mecca than philosophical talking shop, but it remains a Paris institution.

▸P.134 ▸ ST-GERMAIN ◀

Musée Carnavalet

Proust wrote most of his great novel, *A la recherche du temps perdu*, cocooned in his cork-lined bedroom, now reconstructed at the Musée Carnavalet.

▸P.109 ▸ THE MARAIS ▼

Paris views

From **on high**, Paris looks like a sea of nineteenth-century mansion buildings, their pale stone facades turning creamy-golden in the sun. The long boulevards look like leafy canyons and the parks like great green pools, but it's the cemeteries that stand out most of all, studded with pale stone graves that could almost be miniature apartment blocks. There are no skyscrapers to hide the old city centre, so it's easy to pick out the great landmarks, from the towers of Notre-Dame and the giant sculpted swathe of the Louvre to the multicoloured pipes and tubes of the Pompidou Centre.

Georges, Pompidou Centre

Eating is very much a secondary affair here – it's the stunning view of the Paris rooftops that's the real draw.

▶ P.103 ▶ BEAUBOURG AND
LES HALLES

Sacré-Cœur

The steps of the Sacré-Cœur are famously romantic, with Paris spread out below you to the south, and the sun full on your face.

▶ P.155 ▶ MONTMARTRE AND
NORTHERN PARIS

Parc de Belleville

A little out of the way, but worth a trek for the splendid views of the city afforded by the park's heights.

▶P.172 ▶ EASTERN PARIS ▲

Eiffel Tower

The view from the Eiffel Tower is especially spectacular at night when the whole tower is lit up from within, and the searchlight sweeps the skies above.

▶P.130 ▶ EIFFEL TOWER AREA ▲

Arc de Triomphe

Views from the top are best towards dusk on a sunny day when the marble of the Grande Arche de la Défense sparkles in the setting sun and the Louvre is bathed in warm light.

▶P.79 ▶ THE CHAMPS ELYSEES AND TUILERIES ▼

Tour Montparnasse

The vista from the tower-top helipad is stunning, and you can have a drink in the panoramic 56th-floor restaurant afterwards.

▶P.142 ▶ MONTPARNASSE ◀

Medieval Paris

In the second half of the nineteenth century, Baron Haussmann flattened Paris's slums to clear space for the handsome boulevards and grand apartment blocks that now define the cityscape, destroying much of the city's medieval patrimony in the process. The notoriously filthy, narrow medieval streets have completely disappeared – though the touristy area around **rue de la Huchette** preserves something of the old layout – but a few grander monuments have survived. The obvious place to go is **Notre-Dame** cathedral, but there are other, equally beautiful things to see, especially in the historic **Quartier Latin**.

St-Etienne-du-Mont

At St-Etienne-du-Mont you can see an extraordinary clash between the flamboyant Gothic style and the Renaissance architecture of the sixteenth century.

▶ P.121 ▶ QUARTIER LATIN ▼

Musée National du Moyen Age

Set in a fine Renaissance mansion, Paris's Museum of the Middle Ages houses all manner of *objets d'art* including: the captivating tapestry series of *The Lady and the Unicorn*.

▶ P.118 ▶ QUARTIER LATIN ▼

Sainte-Chapelle

The Sainte-Chapelle, with its stunning stained-glass windows, is one of the jewels of the Middle Ages.

▸ P.68 ▸ THE ISLANDS ▲

Conciergerie

The Conciergerie's impressive Gothic halls are among the few surviving vestiges of the original palace that once stood on the Ile de la Cité.

▸ P.70 ▸ THE ISLANDS ▼

The Sorbonne

In medieval times Paris was famous throughout Europe for its university colleges, based on the hilltop on the Seine's left bank. Of these, the Sorbonne is still there.

▸ P.120 ▸ QUARTIER LATIN ▼

Places

Places

The Islands

There's no better place to start a tour of Paris than with its two river islands, Ile de la Cité, the city's ancient core, and charming, village-like Ile St-Louis.

The **Ile de la Cité** is where Paris began. It was settled in around 300 BC by a Celtic tribe, the Parisii, and in 52 BC was overrun by Julius Caesar's troops. The Romans called the settlement Lutetia Parisiorum and turned it into an administrative centre, building a palace-fortress at the western end of the Île de la Cité. In the tenth century the Frankish kings transformed this fortress into a splendid palace, of which the **Sainte-Chapelle** and the **Conciergerie** prison survive today.

At the other end of the island they erected the great cathedral of **Notre-Dame**. It takes some stretch of the imagination today to picture what this medieval settlement must have looked like, for most of it was erased in the nineteenth century by Baron Haussmann, Napoleon III's Préfet de la Seine (a post equivalent to mayor of Paris). Some ninety streets were destroyed and in their place were raised four vast Neoclassical edifices: the Tribunal de Commerce; the Hôtel Dieu; the Préfecture de Police; and an extension to the Palais de Justice. The few corners of the island that escaped Haussmann's attentions include the leafy **square du Vert-Galant** and charming **place Dauphine**.

The smaller **Ile St-Louis** is prime strolling territory. Unlike its larger neighbour, it has no heavyweight sights; rather the island's charm lies in its handsome ensemble of austerely

▼ PONT NEUF

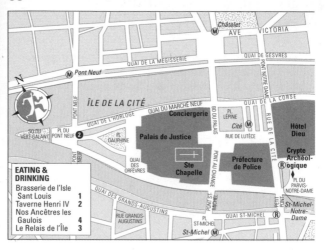

EATING &
DRINKING

Brasserie de l'Isle
Sant Louis   1
Taverne Henri IV   2
Nos Ancêtres les
Gaulois   4
Le Relais de l'Île   3

beautiful seventeenth-century houses, tree-lined *quais* and narrow streets, harbouring restaurants, art galleries and gift shops. For centuries the Ile St-Louis was nothing but swampy pastureland, a haunt of lovers, duellists and miscreants on the run, until in the seventeenth-century the real-estate developer, Christophe Marie, had the bright idea of filling it with elegant mansions. One of the finest is the **Hôtel Lauzun**, which became for a while a favourite meeting place of bohemian writers and artists in the nineteenth century.

Pont Neuf

Despite its name, the Pont Neuf is the city's oldest surviving bridge, built in 1607 by Henri IV, one of the city's first great town planners. A graceful stone construction with twelve arches, the bridge links the western tip of the island with both banks of the river. It was the first in Paris to be made of stone rather than wood, hence the name.

Henri is commemorated with a stately equestrian statue halfway across.

Square du Vert-Galant

Enclosed within the triangular "stern" of the island, the square du Vert-Galant is a tranquil, tree-lined garden and a popular haunt of lovers. The square takes its name (a "Vert-Galant" is a "green" or "lusty" gentleman) from the nickname given to Henri IV, whose amorous exploits were legendary.

Place Dauphine

Red-brick seventeenth-century houses flank the entrance to place Dauphine, one of the city's most secluded and attractive squares, lined with venerable town houses. The noise of traffic recedes here, likely to be replaced by nothing more intrusive than the gentle tap of boules being played in the shade of the chestnuts.

The Sainte-Chapelle

Entrance on bd du Palais. Daily:
March–Oct 9.30am–6pm; Nov–Feb

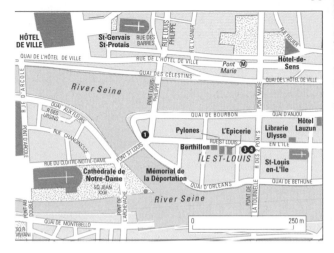

10am–5pm. €6.10, combined admission to the Conciergerie €8. The slender spire of the Sainte-Chapelle soars high above the Palais de Justice buildings. Though damaged in the Revolution, it was sensitively restored in the mid nineteenth century and remains one of the finest achievements of French High Gothic, renowned for its exquisite stained-glass windows.

The building was constructed by Louis IX between 1242 and 1248 to house a collection of holy relics, including Christ's crown of thorns and a fragment of the True Cross, bought from the bankrupt empire of Byzantium. It actually consists of two chapels: the rather dark **lower chapel**, with its star-painted ceiling, was where the servants worshipped, while the **upper chapel** was reserved for the court. The latter is a truly dazzling sight: its walls seem to be made almost entirely of magnificent stained glass, held up by deceptively fragile-looking stone columns. The glowing blues and

reds of the stained glass dapple the interior, giving the impression of being surrounded by myriad brilliant butterflies. The windows, two-thirds of which are original (the others are from the nineteenth-century restora-

▼ SAINTE-CHAPELLE

tion), tell virtually the entire story of the Bible, beginning on the north side with Genesis and various other books of the Old Testament, continuing with the Passion of Christ (east end) and ending with the Apocalypse in the rose window.

The Conciergerie

Entrance on quai de l'Horloge. Daily: March–Oct 9.30am–6pm; Nov–Feb 10am–5pm. €6.10, combined ticket with Sainte-Chapelle €8. Located within the Palais de Justice complex, the Conciergerie is Paris's oldest prison, where Marie-Antoinette and, in their turn, the leading figures of the Revolution were incarcerated before execution. It was turned into a prison – and put in the charge of a "concierge", or steward – after Etienne Marcel's uprising in 1358 led Charles V to decamp to the greater security of the Louvre.

The Conciergerie's entry on quai de l'Horloge is flanked by two fine medieval towers – the one on the right, dating from the thirteenth century, was known as the Bonbec tower, so named because this was where prisoners were tortured and reduced to a *bonbec* ("babbler").

Inside are several splendidly vaulted Gothic halls, among the few surviving vestiges of the original Capetian palace. Elsewhere a number of rooms and prisoners' cells, including Marie-Antoinette's cell, have been reconstructed to show what they might have been like at the time of the French Revolution.

Cathédrale de Notre-Dame

Cathedral: daily 8am–6.45pm, Sun closes at 7.45pm; free. Towers: April–Sept 9.30am–6.45pm, Oct–March 10am–5pm. €6.10. Guided tours: in French Mon–Fri noon & Sat 2pm; in English Wed noon; 60–90min; free; gather at the welcome desk near the entrance. One of the master-pieces of the Gothic age, the Cathédrale de Notre-Dame rears up from the Ile de la Cité like a ship moored by huge fly-ing buttresses. It was among the first of the great Gothic cathe-drals built in northern France and one of the most ambitious, its nave reaching an unprece-dented 33m. Built on the site of the Merovingian cathedral of Saint-Etienne, Notre-Dame was begun in 1160 and completed around 1345. In the seventeenth and eighteenth centuries it fell into decline, suffering its worst depredations during the Revolution when the frieze of Old Testament kings on the facade was damaged by enthusi-asts who mistook them for the kings of France.

It was only in the 1820s that the cathedral was at last given a much-needed restoration, a task entrusted to the great architect-restorer Viollet-le-Duc, who carried out a

▼ CONCIERGERIE

▲ NOTRE-DAME

thorough – some would say too thorough – renovation, remaking much of the statuary on the facade (the originals can be seen in the Musée National du Moyen Age; see p.118) and adding the steeple and baleful-looking gargoyles, which you can see close up if you brave the ascent of the **towers**.

The cathedral's **facade** is one of its most impressive exterior features; the Romanesque influence is still visible, not least in its solid H-shape, but the over-riding impression is one of lightness and grace, created in part by the delicate filigree work of the central rose window and the gallery above. There are some magnificent carvings over the portals; the oldest are those over the right portal depicting the Virgin enthroned, and below, episodes from the life of Saint Anne (Mary's mother) and the life of Christ.

Inside, you're struck by the dramatic contrast between the darkness of the nave and the light falling on the first great clustered pillars of the choir. It's the end walls of the transepts that admit all this light, being nearly two-thirds glass, including two magnificent rose windows coloured in imperial purple. These, the vaulting and the soaring shafts reaching to the springs of the vaults, are all definite Gothic elements, while there remains a strong sense of Romanesque in the stout round pillars of the nave and the general sense of four-squareness.

The kilomètre zéro

On the pavement by the west door of Notre-Dame is a spot, marked by a bronze star, known as kilomètre zéro, from which all main-road distances in France are calculated.

The crypte archéologique

Place du Parvis-Notre-Dame. Tues–Sun 10am–6pm. €3.30. The atmospher-ically lit crypte archéologique is a large excavated area under the place du Parvis revealing the remains of the original cathedral, as well as vestiges of the streets and houses that once clustered around Notre-Dame: most are medieval, but some date as far back as Gallo-Roman times.

Le Mémorial de la Déportation

Daily 10am–noon & 2–5pm. Free. Scarcely visible above ground, the stark and moving Mémorial de la Déportation is the symbolic tomb of the 200,000 French who died in Nazi concentration camps during World War II – Resistance fighters, Jews and forced labourers among them. Stairs hardly shoulder-wide descend into a space like a prison yard and then into a crypt, off which is a long, narrow, stifling corridor, its walls covered in thousands of points of light representing the dead. Above the exit are the words "Forgive. Do not forget."

Hôtel Lauzun

Pre-arranged group visits possible on ☎01.42.76.57.99. The Hôtel Lauzun, built in 1657, has an intact interior, complete with splendid trompe l'oeil decorations. In the 1840s, it was the meeting place for the Haschischins club, whose members included Baudelaire, Balzac and Manet; as the club's name suggests, hashish was handed round – apparently in the form of a green jelly.

▲ LE RELAIS DE L'ISLE

Shops

Berthillon

31 rue St-Louis-en-l'Ile. Wed–Sun 10am–8pm. Long queues form for these exquisite ice creams and sorbets that come in all sorts of unusual fruity flavours, such as rhubarb.

L'Epicerie

51 rue St-Louis-en-l'Ile. Daily 11am–8pm. Beautifully packaged vinegars, oils, jams and mustards, with some unusual flavourings such as orange- and rosemary-flavoured white-wine vinegar from Champagne.

Librairie Ulysse

26 rue St-Louis-en-l'Ile. Tues–Sat 2–8pm. A tiny bookshop, piled from floor to ceiling with new and secondhand travel books and run by a friendly English-speaking owner.

Pylônes

57 rue St-Louis-en-l'Ile. Daily 11am–7.30pm. A gift shop selling weird and wacky knick-knacks and gadgets, including inflatable fruit bowls, grasshopper can crushers and sparkly resin jewellery.

Restaurants

Brasserie de l'Île St-Louis

55 quai de Bourbon. Thurs–Tues noon–midnight. A friendly brasserie with a rustic, dark-wood interior and a sunny terrace, serving moderately priced Alsatian cuisine such as sauerkraut with ham and sausage.

Nos Ancêtres les Gaulois

39 rue St-Louis-en-l'Île ☎01.46.33.66.07. Daily 7pm–2am, plus Sun noon–4pm. A veritable Gaulois (think *Asterix and Obelix*) theme park, with rustic tables and musty animal skins, this restaurant offers a copious all-you-can-eat-and-drink buffet. There's also a children's set meal.

Le Relais de l'Île

37 rue St-Louis-en-l'Île ☎01.46.34.72.34. Mon & Wed–Sun noon–2pm & 7.30–11pm. A cosy, candlelit jazz-restaurant serving decent food, with mains such as rabbit in prune sauce and lemon chicken with honey. It's the convivial ambience that makes this place special: friendly service, the pianist tinkling away and the chef occasionally popping out from the kitchen to join in.

Bars

Taverne Henri IV

13 place du Pont-Neuf. Mon–Fri 11.30am–3.30pm & 6–9pm, Sat noon–4pm; closed Aug. An old-style wine bar, serving reasonably priced wine and snacks, buzziest at lunchtime when lawyers from the nearby Palais de Justice drop in.

Live music

Sainte-Chapelle

Tickets €16–25. ☎01.42.77.65.65; bookings also at any FNAC (see p.166)store or Virgin Megastore. Classical music concerts are held in the splendid surroundings of the chapel more or less daily.

▲ LIVE JAZZ ON THE ILE ST-LOUIS

The Louvre

The Louvre is one of the world's truly great museums. Opened in 1793, during the Revolution, it soon acquired the largest art collection on earth, thanks to Napoleon's conquests. Today, it houses paintings, sculpture and precious art objects, covering everything from Ancient Egyptian jewellery to the beginnings of Impressionism. Even if you're not venturing inside, the palace itself is breathtaking, cutting a grand classical swathe right through the centre of the city.

Quite separate from the Louvre proper, but still within the palace, are three museums under the aegis of the Union **Centrale des Arts Décoratifs**, dedicated to fashion and textiles, decorative arts and advertising.

The palace

For centuries the site of the French court, the palace was originally little more than a feudal fortress, begun by Philippe-Auguste in 1200. In fact, it wasn't until the reign of François I, in the first flowering of the Renaissance, that the foundations of the present-day building were

laid, and from then on almost every sovereign added to the Louvre, leaving the palace a surprisingly harmonious building. Even with the addition in 1989 of the initially controversial glass **Pyramide** in the Cour Napoleon – an extraordinary leap of imagination conceived by the Chinese-born architect I. M. Pei – the overall effect of the Louvre is of a quintessentially French grandeur and symmetry.

Painting

By far the largest of the museum's collections is its paintings. The early **Italians** are perhaps the most interesting, among

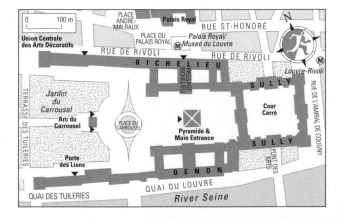

▲ THE LOUVRE PALACE

Francis of Assisi, and Fra Angelico's *Coronation of the Virgin*. Fifteenth- to seventeenth-century Italian paintings line the length of the Grande Galerie. Outstanding works here are Leonardo's *Virgin and child with St Anne* and *Virgin of the Rocks*, several Raphael masterpieces, and Mantegna's *Crucifixion*. Large-scale nineteenth-century French works are displayed in the parallel suite of rooms, among them the epic *Coronation of Napoleon I*, by David, Ingres' languorous nude, *La Grande Odalisque*, and *Géricault's* harrowing *Raft of the Medusa*, which depicts a notorious incident in which shipwrecked sailors on a raft turned to cannibalism.

A good place to start a circuit of **French paintings** is with the master of French Classicism, Poussin; his profound themes, taken from antiquity, the Bible and mythology, together with his harmonious style, were to influence generations of artists.

them Leonardo da Vinci's *Mona Lisa*. If you want to get near her, go first or last thing in the day. Other highlights of the Italian collection include two complete Botticelli frescoes, Giotto's *Stigmatization of St*

Visiting the Louvre

Mon & Wed 9am–9.45pm, Thurs–Sun 9am–6pm. €7.50, or €5 after 3pm & Sun, free first Sun of the month except public hols. Same-day readmission allowed. Ⓦ www.louvre.fr.

Tickets can be bought in advance on ☎ 08.92.68.36.22; online; or from branches of FNAC and Virgin Megastore, as found everywhere in Paris. The **main entrance** is via the Pyramid; if the queues look too long, then try the entrance directly under the Arc du Carrousel, which has secondary access tunnels leading from 99 rue de Rivoli and from the line #1 Palais Royal-Musée du Louvre Métro stop. The Porte des Lions, on the quai des Tuileries, provides another quick way into the museum. Ticket holders can enter from the **Passage Richelieu**, which has views of the dramatically glazed-over sculpture courtyards.

Due to the sheer volume of exhibits (not to mention visitors), even if you spent the entire day here you'd see only a fraction of the collection, so consider confining yourself to a single section of the museum. The **Denon** wing is very popular: as well as the *Mona Lisa*, it houses all of the Italian paintings, some tremendous French nineteenth-century canvases, and the great Italian and Classical sculptures. Rewarding and relatively peaceful alternatives are the grand chronologies of **French painting** and sculpture, or a stroll through the sensual collection of **Objets d'Art**. Wherever you're headed, pick up a free **floor plan** – essential for navigation.

You'll need a healthy appetite for Classicism in the next suite of rooms, but there are some arresting portraits, and the paintings of Georges de la Tour are superbly idiosyncratic. When you move into the rather less severe eighteenth century, the more intimate paintings of Watteau come as a relief, as do Chardin's intense still lifes. In the later part of the collection, the chilly wind of Neoclassicism blows through the paintings of Gros, Gérard, Prud'hon, David and Ingres, contrasting with the more sentimental style that begins with Greuze and continues into the Romanticism of Géricault and Delacroix. The final rooms take in Corot and the Barbizon school, the precursors of Impressionism. The Louvre's collection of French painting stops at 1848, a date picked up by the Musée d'Orsay (see p.132).

In the **Dutch** and **Spanish** collections, works worth lingering over are Rembrandt's superb *Supper at Emmaus*, with its dramatic use of chiaroscuro, Murillo's tender *Beggar Boy*, and the Goya portraits. Interspersed throughout the painting section are rooms dedicated to the Louvre's impressive collection of prints and drawings, exhibited by rotation.

Antiquities

The **Oriental Antiquities** and **Arts of Islam** category covers the Mesopotamian, Sumerian, Babylonian, Assyrian and Phoenician civilizations, and the art of ancient Persia, India and Spain. One of the collection's most important exhibits is the *Code of Hammurabi*, a basalt stele covered in Akkadian script setting down King Hammurabi's rules of conduct for his subjects.

The **Egyptian Antiquities** collection starts with the atmospheric crypt of the Sphinx. Everyday life is illustrated through cooking accessories, jewellery, the principles of hieroglyphics, musical instruments, sarcophagi and a host of mummified cats. The collection

▼ THE COUR MARLY, RICHELIEU WING

▲ COUR NAPOLÉON

rated in the style of Louis-Philippe, the last king of France. Numerous rooms have been partially re-created in the style of a particular epoch, and walking through the complete chronology, where suites are often devoid of other visitors, gives a powerful sense of the evolution of aesthetic taste at its most refined and opulent.

Towards the end, the circuit passes through the breathtaking apartments of Napoleon III's minister of state.

Sculpture

The Sculpture section covers the entire development of the art in France from the Romanesque to Rodin, all in the Richelieu wing, and Italian and northern European sculpture in the Denon wing, including Michelangelo's *Slaves*, designed for the tomb of Pope Julius II. The huge glass-covered courtyards of the Richelieu wing – the cour Marly with the Marly Horses, which once graced place de la Concorde, and the cour Puget with Puget's *Milon de Crotone* as the centrepiece – are very impressive, if a bit overwhelming.

The half-dozen rooms of the Pavillon des Sessions house statuary from **Africa, Asia, Oceania and the Americas**.

Union Centrale des Arts Décoratifs

107 rue de Rivoli. Tues–Fri 11am–6pm, Sat & Sun 10am–6pm. €7. ⓦ www .ucad.fr. The other museums housed in the Louvre under the umbrella organization Union Centrale des Arts Décoratifs can be among the city's most innovative.

The **Musée de la Mode et du Textile** holds high-quality temporary exhibitions demon-

continues with the development of Egyptian art; highlights include the expressive *Seated Scribe* (c.2500 BC) and the huge bust of Amenophis IV (1365–1349 BC).

The biggest crowd-pullers in the museum after the *Mona Lisa* are found in the **Greek and Roman Antiquities** section: the dramatic *Winged Victory of Samothrace*, and the late second-century BC *Venus de Milo*, striking a classic model's pose. Her antecedents are all on display, too, from the graceful marble head of the *Cycladic Idol* and the delightful *Dame d'Auxerre* to the Classical perfection of the *Athlete of Benevento*. The Roman section includes some wonderful frescoes from Pompeii and Herculaneum.

Objets d'Art

The vast Objets d'Art section presents the finest tapestries, ceramics, jewellery and furniture commissioned by France's most wealthy and influential patrons, beginning with the rather pious Middle Ages section and continuing through 81 relentlessly superb rooms to a salon deco-

▲ VIEW FROM INSIDE THE PYRAMID

strating the most brilliant and cutting-edge of Paris fashions from all eras, such as Jackie Kennedy's famous 1960s dresses.

On the top floor, the **Musée de la Publicité** shows off its collection of advertising posters through cleverly themed, temporary exhibitions. The space is appropriately trendy – half exposed brickwork and steel panelling, and half crumbling Louvre finery.

The relatively traditional **Musée des Arts Décoratifs** seems something of the odd man out, though its eclectic collection of art and superbly crafted furniture fits the Union Centrale's "design" theme. The medieval and Renaissance rooms show off curiously shaped and beautifully carved chairs, dressers and tables, religious paintings, and Venetian glass. There are also some wonderful tapestries – including the delightful late-fifteenth-century *Le Berger*, depicting a shepherd surrounded by a very woolly flock – and a room decorated and furnished entirely as a late-medieval bedroom. Changing

contemporary collections display works by French, Italian and Japanese designers, including some great examples of the work of Philippe Starck.

Cafés

Café Richelieu

First floor, Richelieu wing. The soigné decor makes this the most prim and elegant of the Louvre's cafés, with full meals available as well as drinks and snacks.

Café Denon

Lower ground floor, Denon wing. It's worth seeking out this cosy little tearoom and restaurant, hidden away among the Louvre's vaults.

Café Mollien

First floor, Denon wing. The busiest of the Louvre's cafés has a prime position near the Grande Galerie, with huge windows giving onto a terrace (in summer) overlooking the Pyramide.

▼ SCULPTURAL DETAIL, LOUVRE PALACE

The Champs-Elysées and Tuileries

The breathtakingly ambitious Champs-Elysées is part of a grand, nine-kilometre axis, often referred to as the "Voie Triomphale", or Triumphal Way, that extends from the Louvre at the heart of the city to the Défense business district in the west. Combining imperial pomp and supreme elegance, it offers impressive vistas along its entire length and incorporates some of the city's most famous landmarks – the place de la Concorde, Tuileries gardens and the Arc de Triomphe. The whole ensemble is so regular and geometrical it looks as though it might have been laid out by a single town planner rather than successive kings, emperors and presidents, all keen to add their stamp and promote French power and prestige.

The Champs-Elysées

Scene of the annual Bastille Day procession, the Champs-Elysées is the nation's best-known avenue. Its heyday was during the Second Empire when members of the *haute bourgeoisie* built themselves splendid mansions along its length and fashionable society frequented the avenue's cafés and theatres. Nowadays, tree-lined and broad, it looks at its most impressive from a distance, thanks to its constant traffic and rather anonymous food and retail outlets. Yet some of the avenue's former glitz lives on at places such as the *Lido* cabaret and *Fouquet's* brasserie (which hosts the annual César film awards), while fresh glamour is constantly being injected by chic designer shops, such as Louis Vuitton, and new, fashionable restaurants and bars in the streets that spar off the avenue.

The Arc de Triomphe

Daily: April–Sept 10am–11pm; Oct–March 10am–10.30pm, €7.

Crowning the Champs-Elysées, the Arc de Triomphe sits imposingly in the middle of place Charles de Gaulle, better known as l'Etoile ("star") on account of the twelve avenues, laid out by Haussmann, radiating from it. Modelled on the ancient Roman triumphal arch-

▼ L'ETOILE AND THE CHAMPS-ELYSÉES

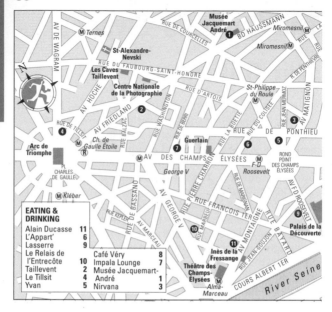

EATING & DRINKING

Alain Ducasse	11		
L'Appart'	6		
Lasserre	9		
Le Relais de		Café Véry	8
l'Entrecôte	10	Impala Lounge	7
Taillevent	2	Musée Jacquemart-	
Le Tillsit	4	André	1
Yvan	5	Nirvana	3

es, this imperial behemoth was built by Napoleon as a homage to the armies of France and is engraved with the names of 660 generals and numerous French battles. The best of the exterior

▼ THE ARC DE TRIOMPHE

reliefs is François Rude's *Marseillaise*, in which a terrifying Amazon-type figure personifying the Revolution charges forward with a sword, her face contorted in a fierce rallying cry. A quiet reminder of the less glorious side of war is the **tomb of the unknown soldier** placed beneath the arch and marked by an eternal flame that is stoked up every evening by war veterans. The climb up to the top is well worth it for the panoramic **views**.

The Grand Palais

Galeries nationales du Grand Palais: daily except Tues 10am–8pm, Wed till 10pm. €9. ⓦ www.rmn.fr/galeries nationalesdugrandpalais. Rising above the greenery at the lower end of the Champs-Elysées is the Grand Palais, a gigantic building with a grandiose Neoclassical exterior, glass roofs

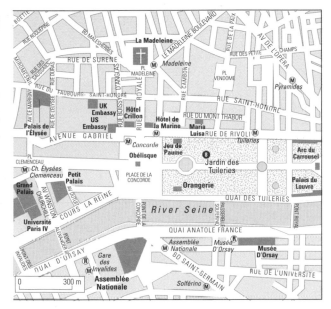

and exuberant flying statuary, created for the 1900 Exposition Universelle. Though part of the building is undergoing renovation, its exhibition space, the **Galeries nationales**, remains unaffected and is Paris's prime venue for major retrospectives of artists such as Chagall, Gauguin and Matisse.

Palais de la Découverte

Main entrance on av Franklin D. Roosevelt. Tues–Sat 9.30am–6pm, Sun & hols 10am–7pm. Museum €5.60, museum and planetarium €8.70. Ⓦ www.palais-decouverte.fr.

Occupy-
ing the west wing of the Grand Palais is Paris's original science museum, dating from the late 1930s. It does an excellent job of bringing science alive – using audiovisual material, models and interactive exhibits. The exhibitions cover chemistry, physics, biology, earth sciences and astronomy, and explore pressing issues such as climate change and biotechnology. There's also an excellent planetarium.

The Petit Palais

The Petit Palais houses the Musée des Beaux-Arts, which comes out of a major revamp at the end of 2004 freeing up more of its gallery space for its extensive holdings. The collection, encompassing every period from the Renaissance to the 1920s, includes some real gems, such as

Monet's *Sunset at Lavacourt* and Boudin's *Gust of Wind at Le Havre*. There's also fantasy jewellery of the Art Nouveau period, effete eighteenth-century furniture and vast canvases recording Paris's street battles during the 1830 and 1848 revolutions.

Musée Jacquemart-André

158 bd Haussmann. Daily 10am–6pm.
€8. ⓦ www.musee-jacquemart
-andre.com. The Musée
Jacquemart-André is set in a magnificent nineteenth-century *hôtel particulier* (mansion), hung with the superb artworks accumulated on the travels of banker Edouard André and his wife, former society portraitist Nélie Jacquemart. A stunning distillation of fifteenth- and sixteenth-century Italian genius, including works by Tiepolo, Botticelli, Donatello, Mantegna and Uccello, forms the core of the

▲ PLACE DE LA CONCORDE

collection. Almost as compelling as the splendid interior and paintings is the insight gleaned into grand nineteenth-century lifestyle.

Place de la Concorde

The vast place de la Concorde has a much less peaceful history than its name suggests. Between 1793 and 1795, some 1300 people died here beneath the Revolutionary guillotine, Louis XVI, Marie-Antoinette, Danton and Robespierre among them. Today, constantly circumnavigated by traffic, the centrepiece of the *place* is a stunning, gold-tipped **obelisk** from the temple of Ramses at Luxor, offered as a favour-currying gesture by the viceroy of Egypt in 1829. From the centre of the square there are sweeping vistas in all directions: the Champs-Elysées looks particularly impressive and you can also admire the alignment of the Assemblée Nationale, in the south, with the church of the Madeleine – both sporting identical Neoclassical facades – at the end of rue Royale, to the north.

▼ PLACE DE LA CONCORDE FROM TUILERIES

Jardin des Tuileries

Daily: April–Sept 7.30am–9pm;
July–Aug 7.30am–11.45pm;
Oct–March 7.30am–7.30pm. The
Jardin des Tuileries, the formal

French garden *par excellence*, dates back to the 1570s, when Catherine de Médicis had the site cleared of the medieval warren of tilemakers (*tuileries*) to make way for a palace and grounds. One hundred years later, Louis XIV commissioned André Le Nôtre to redesign them, and the results are largely what you see today: straight avenues, formal flowerbeds and splendid vistas.

The grand central alley is lined with shady, clipped chestnuts and manicured lawns, and framed at each end by ornamental pools, surrounded by an impressive gallery of copies of statues by the likes of Rodin and Coysevox; you can see the originals in the Louvre. Set in a far corner of the gardens, the **Orangerie**, housing a private art collection, including eight of Monet's giant waterlily paintings, is currently closed for renovation.

Jeu de Paume

Tues 10am–9.30pm, Wed–Fri noon–7pm, Sat & Sun 10am–7pm. €6. The Jeu de Paume, within the Jardin des Tuileries, was once a royal tennis court and later the place where French Impressionist paintings were displayed before being transferred to the Musée d'Orsay. In a subsequent renovation, huge windows were cut into the Jeu de Paume's classical temple walls, allowing light to flood in, and it's now one of the city's best exhibition spaces for contemporary art – usually major retrospectives of established artists.

Shops

Les Caves Taillevent

199 rue du Faubourg St-Honoré. Mon 2pm–8pm, Tues–Fri 9am–7.30pm. An offshoot of the *Taillevent* restaurant, this is a wine connoisseur's paradise, with more than 400,000 bottles from all over France and abroad. Prices start from around €5 a bottle and there are also daily tasting sessions.

Guerlain

68 av des Champs-Elysées. Mon–Sat 10.30am–8pm, Sun 3–7pm. A beautiful *belle époque* boutique selling heady perfumes from the Guerlain range.

Maria Luisa

2 rue Cambon; menswear 38 rue du Mont-Thabor. Mon–Sat 10.30am–7pm. A one-stop shop for cutting-edge designer-wear (Galliano, Balenciaga and the like), often at discounted prices.

Inès de la Fressange

14 av Montaigne. Mon–Sat 10am–7pm. Located on Paris's most exclusive shopping street, this is Inès de la Fressange's flagship store, carrying her elegant clothes and accessories.

▼ JARDIN DES TUILERIES

Cafés

Café Véry (Dame Tartine)

Jardin des Tuileries. Mon–Fri
9.15am–7pm, Sat & Sun 9.15am–
7.30pm; closed Tues in July & Aug.
The best of a number of café-
restaurants in the garden. Serves
inexpensive snacks as well as
more substantial meals.

Musée Jacquemart-André

158 bd Haussmann. Daily 11.30am–
5.30pm. Admire ceiling frescoes
by Tiepolo while savouring fine
pastries in this sumptuously
appointed *salon de thé* in the
Musée Jacquemart-André.

Restaurants

Alain Ducasse at the Plaza-Athénée

Hotel Plaza-Athénée, 25 av Montaigne
☎01.53.67.65.00. Mon–Fri 1–2.30pm
& 8–10.30pm. Reckoned to be
one of the world's top haute-
cuisine temples, run by star chef
Alain Ducasse; his sublime dishes are likely to revive even the
most jaded palate. The decor is
Louis XV with a modern gloss
and the service – as you'd
expect – is impeccable. Reckon
on €160 upwards and book
well in advance.

L'Appart'

9 rue du Colisée ☎01.53.75.16.34.
Restaurant: daily noon–2.30pm &
7.30–11pm; bar daily noon to midnight, Sun & Mon till 11pm. Drawing
a young, trendy crowd, this is a
stylish place, with a huge bar
downstairs and a restaurant
upstairs resembling an elegant
living room, with wood panelling, fireplaces and deep-red
fabrics. Moderately expensive,
classic French dishes.

Lasserre

17 av Franklin D. Roosevelt
☎01.43.59.53.43. Mon–Fri noon–2pm
& 7.30–10pm. A classic haute-cui-

▼ MUSÉE JACQUEMART-ANDRÉ SALON DE THÉ

sine restaurant with a lovely *belle époque* dining room and a roof that's rolled back on balmy summer days. *A la carte* prices are expensive, though you can eat more cheaply at lunchtime if you opt for the set menu.

Le Relais de l'Entrecôte

15 rue Marbeuf. Noon–2.30pm & 7.30–11pm. *Le Relais de l'Entrecôte*, which roughly translates as "Steaks R us", has only one dish on the menu: steak and *frites*. This is no ordinary steak though – the secret is in the delicious sauce. Prices are reasonable for the area.

Taillevent

15 rue Lamennais ☎01.44.95.15.01. Mon–Fri 12.30–2.30pm & 7.30–11.30pm. One of Paris's finest gourmet restaurants. The Provençal-influenced cuisine and wine list are exceptional, the decor classy and refined. Reckon on an average of €150 a head, excluding wine, and book well in advance.

Le Tillsit

14 rue de Tillsit. Daily 7am–midnight. A stone's throw away from the Arc de Triomphe and sporting a gaudy glass centrepiece, this otherwise unassuming brasserie is a locals' favourite and fills up quickly at lunchtime.

Yvan

1 bis rue J-Mermoz; ☎01.43.59.18.40. Mon–Fri noon–2.30pm & 8pm–midnight, Sat eve only. An elegant restaurant with deep-red, plush interior. The excellent food includes many Belgian specialities, such as *moules frites*. Three courses cost around €30 and it's best to book ahead.

Bars

Impala Lounge

2 rue de Berri. Daily till 4am. A trendy, *Out of Africa*-themed bar, with great atmosphere and music – mostly reggae, funk and afro-jazz.

Nirvana

3 av Matignon. Daily till 4am. A hip bar-restaurant/club with Indian-inspired decor where well-known DJ Claude Challe and guest celebrities spin the discs.

Live music

Théâtre des Champs-Elysées

15 av Montaigne ☎01.49.52.50.50, ❀www.theatredeschampselysees.com. Built in 1913, this historic theatre, where Stravinsky premiered his *Rite of Spring*, is home to the Orchestre National de France and also hosts many international concerts and ballets. Tickets are as cheap as €5 for a seat with no view, otherwise they range from €12 to €115.

PLACES The Champs-Elysées and Tuileries

Trocadéro

The swish little strip of the 16e arrondissement that runs alongside the Seine is unusually thick with good museums, even for Paris. Between place de l'Alma, notorious as the scene of Princess Diana's fatal car crash, and place du Trocadéro, from which the area gets its name, stretch broad, leafy and largely residential boulevards, lined with the homes of wealthy Parisians and their expensive little dogs. The atmosphere of the quarter isn't exactly lively, but the views across the river to the Eiffel Tower and the 7e arrondissement are wonderful, especially from the terrace of the Palais de Chaillot.

Palais de Chaillot

From behind its elaborate park and fountains, the sweeping arcs of the Palais de Chaillot seem designed to embrace the view of the Eiffel Tower, which stands on the far side of the river. The rather brutal Modernist-Classical architecture dates the palace to 1937, when it was built as the showpiece of the Exposition Universelle, one of Paris's regular trade and culture jamborees. In recent years the palace has acquired a forlorn air, housing just a pair of low-key museums (see below) and the stage of the radical Théâtre National de Chaillot, but the central terrace between the palace's two wings still forms a perfect platform for photo opportunities and curio-sellers.

▼ PALAIS DE CHAILLOT

Cité de l'Architecture et du Patrimoine

Palais de Chaillot. Opens 2005. The completion of the Cité de l'Architecture et du Patrimoine will help bring the Palais de Chaillot back to life. This combined institute, library and museum of architecture will display giant-sized plaster casts taken from great French buildings, designed to tell the story of French architecture from the Middle Ages through to the nineteenth century. More modern buildings will be served by photographs, designs and original architectural models.

Musée de l'Homme

Palais de Chaillot. Mon & Wed–Sun 9.45am–5.15pm; closed public hols. €7. In 2002, President Chirac robbed the Musée de l'Homme of almost all of its ethnographical pieces for his giant museum of world folk art across the river on quai Branly. All that's left now are the relatively worthy anthropological exhibits – tools, textiles, implements, religious artefacts – and the large collection of musical instruments, which continue to edify schoolchildren and intrigue a few curious visitors.

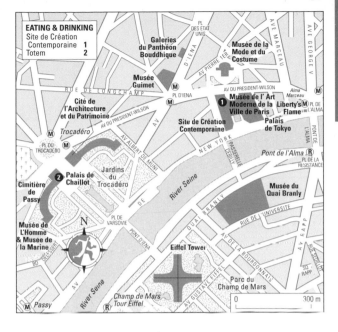

Musée de de la Marine

Palais de Chaillot. Mon & Wed–Sun
10am–6pm. €7. www.musee
-marine.fr. The Musée de de la
Marine is worth visiting for its
beautiful, super-scale models of
French ships. These range from
ancient galleys to Napoleonic
three-deckers, and from giant
trawlers to the latest nuclear
submarines.

Musée Guimet

Place d'Iéna. Mon & Wed–Sun
10am–6pm. €5.50. www.musee
guimet.fr. Galeries du Panthéon
Bouddhique entrance at 19 avenue
d'Iéna. The airy, light-filled atrium of the Musée National des
Arts Asiatiques-Guimet is peo-
pled with exquisite Buddha
statues and figurines from
Cambodia's ancient Khmer
dynasty. It's a breathtaking
introduction to the museum's

world-renowned collection of
Buddhist and Asian art. Above,
the museum winds round four
floors groaning with
dramatically lit statues of
Buddhas and gods.

On the third floor, the rotunda
was used by the collection's
founder, **Emile Guimet**, for
the first Buddhist ceremony
ever held in France. A great
collector and patron of the arts,
he came from a family of enor-
mously wealthy industrialists.
His original collection, brought
back from his travels in Asia in
1876, is exhibited in the nearby
Galeries du Panthéon
Bouddhique.

Musée de la Mode et du Costume

Palais Galliera. Tues–Sun 10am–6pm.
01.56.52.86.00. €7. The
grandiose Palais Galliera is home

▲ MUSEE D'ART MODERNE DE LA VILLE DE PARIS

to the Musée de la Mode et du Costume, which runs two or three major exhibitions of clothes and fashion each year, drawing from the museum's exceptional collection. Themes range from the work of individual *couturiers* to historical shows looking at the style of a particular era. During changeovers the museum is closed, so call in advance to check – the staff speak English.

Musée d'Art Moderne de la Ville de Paris

Palais de Tokyo. Tues–Fri 10am–5.45pm, Sat & Sun 10am–6.45pm; closed public hols. Under renovation until 2005. Free. The Musée d'Art Moderne de la Ville de Paris displays the city's own collection of modern art. It may not rival the Pompidou Centre for super-celebrity works, but many of the paintings have a rewarding Parisian theme, and the setting in the elegant, Modernist Palais de Tokyo is perfect, as there's a strong collection of early twentieth-century artists – notably Braque, Chagall, Delaunay, Derain, Léger, Modigliani and Picasso. Highlights are the chapel-like

salle Matisse, devoted to Matisse's *La Danse de Paris*, and Dufy's enormous mural *La Fée Electricité* (*The Electricity Fairy*), which fills an entire, curved room with 250 lyrical, colourful panels recounting the story of electricity from Aristotle to the the 1930s. The collection is kept up to the minute by an active buying policy, and the visit usually ends with the latest video acquisition or installation.

In the courtyard garden you can have a drink and admire the smooth columns framing a view of the Eiffel Tower.

Site de Création Contemporaine

Palais de Tokyo. Tues–Sun noon –midnight. Cost varies. ⓦwww .palaisdetokyo.com. The semi-derelict interior of the Palais de Tokyo's western wing looks as if it has been hit by a bomb, with its wires and concrete beams and pipes haphazardly exposed. The effect is in fact deliberate, an avant-garde "anti-museum" statement made by the building's occupants: the Site de Création Contemporaine. This is the French state's chief space for cutting-edge contemporary art

---

events, with a constant flow of French conceptual art shows. Paris-born Louise Bourgeois has exhibited here, and the site has been occupied – with official sanction – by groups as diverse as a squat-living art collective and a posse of skateboard artistes.

Place de l'Alma

From most angles, place de l'Alma looks like just another busy Parisian junction, with cars rattling over the cobbles and a Métro entrance on the pavement. Over in one corner, however, stands a replica of the flame from the Statue of Liberty, which was given to France in 1987 as a symbol of Franco-American relations.

This golden torch has now been adopted by mourners from all over the world as a memorial to Princess Diana, who was killed in the underpass beneath in 1997. A low wall is covered

▲ SITE DE CREATION CAFE

with loving graffiti messages, though they're periodically cleaned off by the disapproving authorities.

Cafés

Site de Création Contemporaine

Palais de Tokyo. Tues–Sun noon–midnight. This café and restaurant inside the gallery are self-consciously hip places to hang out – the Benetton-bright decor of both venues is actually the gallery's permanent art collection. The rather expensive Restaurant du Palais de Tokyo serves cool, modern Mediterranean and fusion flavours, while the downstairs café is a good bet for a drink and a snack.

Totem

Palais de Chaillot. Daily noon–2am. Avoid the tacky, native-American-themed restaurant, and just walk through to the terrace at the back, where you can enjoy magnificent views of the Eiffel Tower over a coffee or a glass of wine.

▼ PLACE DE L'ALMA FLAME

The Grands Boulevards and passages

Built on the old city ramparts, the Grands Boulevards are the eight broad streets that extend in a long arc from the Eglise de la Madeleine eastwards. In the nineteenth century, the boulevards were where *Paris vivant* was to be found, from the fashionable cafés in the west to the more colourful eastern end, with its street theatre and puppet shows. There's nothing that remarkable about the boulevards these days, but vestiges of their past live on in the brasseries, cafés, theatres and cinemas (notably the splendid Art Deco cinemas Rex and Max Linder see p.207).

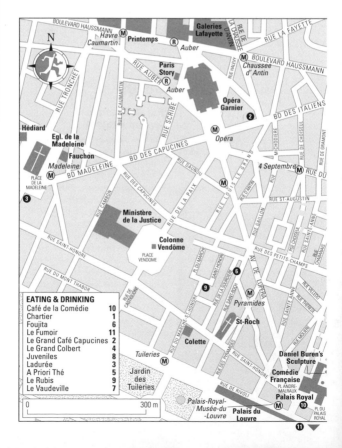

EATING & DRINKING	
Café de la Comédie	10
Chartier	1
Foujita	6
Le Fumoir	11
Le Grand Café Capucines	2
Le Grand Colbert	4
Juveniles	8
Ladurée	3
A Priori Thé	5
Le Rubis	9
Le Vaudeville	7

To the south of the Grands Boulevards lies the city's main commercial and financial district. Right at its heart stand the solid institutions of the Banque de France and the Bourse, while just to the north, beyond the glittering Opéra Garnier, are the large department stores Galeries Lafayette and Printemps. Rather more well-heeled shopping is concentrated on the rue St-Honoré in the west and the streets around aristocratic place Vendôme, lined with top couturiers, jewellers and art dealers. Scattered around the whole area are the delightful **passages** – nineteenth-century arcades that hark back to shopping from a different era.

In the south, the tranquil Palais Royal arcades and gardens make for a perfect rest-stop and are a handy shortcut through to the Bibliothèque Nationale.

Musée Grévin

Bd Montmartre. Daily 10am–5.30pm. €16, children €9. A remnant from the fun-loving times on the Grands Boulevards are the waxworks in the Musée Grévin, comprising mainly French

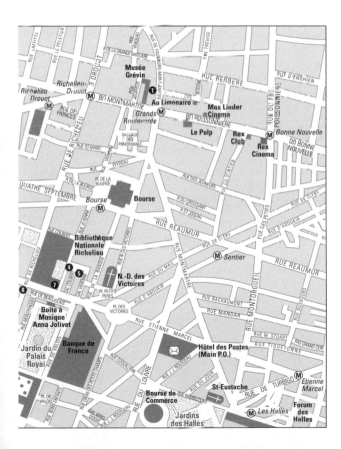

▲ GALLERIES LAFAYETTE ON BOULEVARD HAUSSMANN

personalities and the usual bunch of Hollywood actors. The best thing about the museum are the original rooms: the magical Palais des Mirages (Hall of Mirrors), built for the Exposition Universelle in 1900; the theatre with its sculptures by Bourdelle; and the 1882 Baroque-style Hall of Columns, where among other unlikely juxtapositions, Lara Croft prepares for action a few feet away from a dignified Charles de Gaulle, while Voltaire smiles across at the billowing skirts of Marilyn Monroe.

Opéra Garnier

Daily 10am–5pm. €6. See p.98 for booking information. The fantastically ornate Opéra Garnier, built by Charles Garnier for Napoleon III, exemplifies the Second Empire in its show of wealth and hint of vulgarity. The theatre's facade is a fairytale concoction of white, pink and green marble, colonnades, rearing horses, winged angels and gleaming gold busts. No less opulent is the interior with its spacious, gilded-marble and mirrored lobbies. The auditorium itself is all red velvet and gold leaf, hung with a six-tonne chandelier; the colourful ceiling was painted by Chagall in 1964 and depicts scenes from well-known operas and ballets jumbled up with famous Parisian landmarks. You can visit the interior, including the auditorium, as long as there are no rehearsals (your best chance is between 1 & 2pm).

▲ OPÉRA GARNIER

Paris-Story

11 bis rue Scribe. Shows daily on the hour 9am–7pm. €8. Paris-Story is a multi-media show tracing the history of Paris – it's a brief and highly romanticized overview, but quite enjoyable all the same. The 45-minute film, "narrated" by Victor Hugo, with simultaneous translation in English, uses a kaleidoscope of computer-generated images and archive footage, set against a luscious classical-music soundtrack.

Eglise de la Madeleine

Mon–Sat 7.30am–7pm, Sun 8am–1pm & 4–7pm. See p.98 for concert information. The imperious-looking Eglise de la Madeleine is the parish church of the cream of Parisian high society. Originally intended as a monument to Napoleon's army, it's modelled on a Greek classical temple and is surrounded by Corinthian columns and fronted by a huge pediment depicting *The Last Judgement*. Inside, Charles Marochetti's theatrical sculpture *Mary Magdalene Ascending to Heaven* draws your eye to the high altar. The church's interior is otherwise rather heavy, but if you're lucky, you may hear the organ, reckoned to be one of Paris's best.

Place de la Madeleine

Flower market Tues–Sat 8am–7.30pm. Surrounding the church, place de la Madeleine is home to some of Paris's top gourmet food stores, best-known of which are Fauchon and Hédiard. On the east side is one of the city's oldest flower markets dating back to 1832, while nearby, some rather fine Art Nouveau public toilets are definitely worth inspecting.

Place Vendôme

Built by Versailles architect Hardouin-Mansart, place Vendôme is one of the city's most impressive set pieces. It's a pleasingly symmetrical, eight-sided *place*, enclosed by a harmonious ensemble of elegant mansions, graced with Corinthian pilasters and steeply pitched roofs. Once the grand residences of tax collectors and financiers, they now house such luxury establishments as the *Ritz* hotel, Cartier, Bulgari and other top-flight jewellers, lending the square a decidedly exclusive air. No. 12, now occupied by Chaumet jewellers, is where Chopin died, in 1849.

Somewhat out of proportion with the rest of the square, the centrepiece is a towering triumphal **column**, surmounted by a statue of Napoleon dressed as Caesar. It was raised in 1806 to celebrate the Battle of Austerlitz and features bronze reliefs of scenes of the battle, cast from 1200 recycled Austro-Russian cannons, spiralling their way up.

▼ PLACE VENDOME

94

▲ PALAIS ROYAL

brothels and funfair attractions until the prohibition on public gambling in 1838 put an end to the fun. Folly, some might say, has returned – in the form of contemporary artist Daniel Buren's black-and-white striped pillars, rather like sticks of Brighton rock, all of varying heights, dotted about the main courtyard in front of the palace.

Rue St-Honoré

Rue St-Honoré – especially its western end and its faubourg extension – is a preserve of top fashion designers and art galleries. In recent years newer, cutting-edge designers have begun colonizing the stretch between rue Cambon and rue des Pyramides – a trend that started with the ultra-cool *Hôtel Costes* (see p.192) in the late 1990s, followed by the concept store, Colette (see p.96).

Palais Royal

Gardens daily dawn–dusk. Free. The Palais Royal was built for Cardinal Richelieu in 1624, though little now remains of the original palace. The current building, mostly dating from the eighteenth century, houses various governmental bodies and the Comédie Française, long-standing venue for the classics of French theatre. To the rear lie sedate gardens with fountains and avenues of clipped limes, bounded by stately eighteenth-century mansions built over arcades housing mainly antique and designer shops. You'd hardly guess that for a time these peaceful arcades and gardens were a site of gambling dens,

Galerie Véro-Dodat

Between rue Croix-des-Petits-Champs and rue Jean-Jacques Rousseau. With its tiled floors, ceiling decorations and mahogany shop fronts divided by faux marble columns, Galerie Véro-Dodat is one of the most attractive and homogeneous *passages*. There are some lovely old shops here, such as Monsieur Capia at no. 26, piled high with an impressive collection of antique dolls and miscellaneous curios.

Galerie Vivienne

Links rue Vivienne with rue des Petits-Champs. The flamboyant decor of Grecian and marine motifs of charming Galerie Vivienne establishes the perfect ambience in which to buy Jean-Paul Gaultier gear, or you can browse in the antiquarian bookshop, Librairie Jousseaume, which dates back to the *passage*'s earliest days.

Passage des Panoramas

Off rue Vivienne. The grid of arcades collectively known as the passage des Panoramas has an appealing old-fashioned chic. Standing out among the bric-a-brac shops, stamp and second-hand postcard dealers are a brasserie, *L'Arbre à Cannelle*,

The passages

Conceived by town planners in the early nineteenth century to protect pedestrians from mud and horse-drawn vehicles, the **passages**, elegant glass-roofed shopping arcades, were for decades left to crumble and decay, but many have recently been renovated and restored to something approaching their former glory, and chic boutiques have moved in alongside the old-fashioned traders and secondhand dealers. Most are closed at night and on Sundays.

with fantastic carved wood panelling, and a fine old printshop with its original 1867 fittings.

Passages Jouffroy and Verdeau

Off bd Montmartre.
Across boulevard Montmartre, passage Jouffroy is full of the kind of stores that make shopping an adventure rather than a chore. A M. Segas sells eccentric walking canes and theatrical antiques opposite a shop stocking every conceivable fitting and furnishing for a doll's house, while near the romantic *Hôtel Chopin* (reviewed on p.193), Paul Vulin spreads his secondhand books along the passageway, and Ciné-Doc appeals to cinephiles with its collection of old film posters. Crossing rue de la Grange Batelière, you enter

▼ GALERIE VIVIENNE

passage Verdeau, where old postcard and camera dealers trade alongside smart new art galleries.

Passage du Grand-Cerf

Between rue St-Denis and rue Dessoubs. The three-storey Grand-Cerf is stylistically the best of all the *passages*. The wrought-iron work, glass roof and plain-wood shop fronts have all been cleaned, attracting stylish arts, crafts and contemporary design shops.

Bibliothèque Nationale Richelieu

☎01.79.53.79, ⓦ www.bnf.fr, Exhibitions Tues–Sat 10am–7pm, Sun noon–7pm; €5. Cabinet des Monnaies, Médailles et Antiques Mon–Fri 1–5.45pm, Sat 1–4.45pm, Sun noon–6pm; free. The Bibliothèque Nationale Richelieu, the French National Library, is a huge, forbidding-looking building, dating back to the 1660s. Visiting its temporary exhibitions will give you access to some of the more beautiful parts of the building – the Galerie Mazarine in particular, with its panelled ceilings painted by Romanelli. You can also see a rich and absorbing display of coins and ancient treasures in the Cabinet des Monnaies, Médailles et Antiques. There's no restriction on entering the library, nor on peering into the atmospheric reading rooms, though it's now mostly bereft of books.

Shops

As well as the shops below be sure to check out the *passages* (see p.95), fertile hunting ground for curios and one-off buys.

Boîte à Musique Anna Jolivet

9 rue de Beaujolais, Jardin du Palais Royal. Mon–Sat 10am–7pm. A delightful, minuscule shop selling every style of music box, from inexpensive self-winding toy models to grand cabinets costing thousands of euros.

Colette

213 rue St-Honoré. Mon–Sat 10.30am–7.30pm. This cutting-edge concept store, combining high fashion and design, is as cool as it comes. When you've finished sizing up the Pucci underwear, Stella McCartney fashion and Sonia Rykiel handbags, head for the *Water Bar*, with its eighty different kinds of bottled H_2O.

Fauchon

24–30 place de la Madeleine. Mon–Sat 9.30am–7pm. A cornucopia of extravagant and beautiful groceries, charcuterie and wines. Just the place for presents of tea, jam, truffles, chocolates, exotic vinegars and mustards.

Galeries Lafayette

40 bd Haussmann. Mon–Sat 9.30am–7pm, Thurs till 9pm. This venerable department store's forte is high fashion, with two floors given over to the latest creations by leading designers. Then there's household stuff, a host of big names in men's and women's accessories, a sizeable lingerie department and a huge *parfumerie* – all under a superb 1900 dome.

Hédiard

21 place de la Madeleine. Mon–Sat 8am–10pm. Since the 1850s, the aristocrat's grocer, selling superlative-quality food.

Printemps

64 bd Haussmann. Mon–Sat 9.30am–7pm, Thurs till 10pm. Books, records, a *parfumerie* and an excellent fashion department for women spread over five floors. The sixth-floor restaurant is right underneath the beautiful Art Nouveau glass dome.

Cafés

A Priori Thé

35 Galerie Vivienne. Mon–Sat 9am–6pm, Sun 12.30–6.30pm. In one of the most picturesque *passages*, this inviting café/*salon de thé* serves excellent tea and cakes, as well as more substantial dishes.

Juveniles

47 rue de Richelieu. Mon–Sat noon–11pm. A very popular, tiny wine bar run by a Scot. A great selection of wines from €13 a bottle; reasonably priced snacks and *plats du jour*, too.

Café de la Comédie

153 rue St-Honoré. Tues–Sun 10am–midnight. A small, traditional café opposite the Comédie Française, serving excellent *tartines* (open sandwiches) and *croque-monsieurs*.

▼ MUSIC BOXES AT ANNA JOILET

Ladurée

16 rue Royale. Mon–Sat 8.30am–7pm.
A luxury *salon de thé*, decorated
with gilt-edged mirrors and ceiling frescoes and famous for its
melt-in-your-mouth macaroons.

Restaurants

Chartier

7 rue du Faubourg-Montmartre. Daily
11.30am–3pm & 6–10pm. Brown
linoleum floor, dark-stained
woodwork, brass hat-racks,
waiters in long aprons – the
original decor of an early
twentieth-century soup
kitchen. Worth seeing and,
though crowded and rushed,
the food here is very cheap
and good value.

Foujita

41 rue St-Roche ☎01.42.61.42.93.
Mon–Sat noon–2.15pm & 7.30–10pm;
closed mid-Aug. Quick and crowded, this is one of the cheaper
but better Japanese restaurants,
as shown by the numbers of
Japanese eating here.

Le Grand Café Capucines

4 bd des Capucines. Daily 24hr. A
popular post-cinema/opera
spot with over-the-top, *belle
époque* decor and excellent, if
pricey, seafood.

Le Grand Colbert

Passage Colbert, rue Vivienne,
☎01.42.86.87.88. Daily noon–3pm &
7.30pm–1am; closed mid-July to
mid-Aug. Senior librarians and
academics from the nearby
Bibliothèque Nationale retire
to this elegant *belle époque*
brasserie for lunch, and the-
atregoers drop in later for solid
French cooking. There's a
good-value, all-day set menu,
which includes coffee.

Le Vaudeville

29 rue Vivienne ☎01.40.20.04.62.
Daily 7am–2am. There's often a
queue to get a table at this lively, late-night brasserie, attractively decorated with marble and
mosaics and serving fine cuisine
at slightly above-average prices.

Bars

Le Fumoir

6 rue de l'Amiral-Coligny. Daily
11am–2am. Animated chatter
rises above a mellow jazz
soundtrack and the sound of
cocktail shakers in this coolly
designed and relaxing bar-
restaurant. There's also a library
at the back and foreign newspapers to browse.

Le Rubis

10 rue du Marché-St-Honoré. Mon–Fri
7.30am–10pm, Sat 9am–3pm; closed
mid-Aug. This very small and
crowded wine bar is one of the
oldest in Paris, known for its
excellent wines and homemade
rillettes (a kind of pork pâté).

Clubs

Le Pulp

25 bd Poissonnière ☎01.40.26.01.93,
🌐pulp.xroot.com. Wed–Sat 11.30pm
–6am; Fri & Sat €10, free Wed & Thurs.
Primarily a lesbian club, but its
mixed evenings on Wed and
especially Thurs (electric night)
are tremendously popular and
draw an eclectic crowd.

▼ VIEW OF THE LOUVRE FROM LE FUMOIR

Rex Club

5 bd Poissonnière ☎01.42.36.28.83;
Wed–Sat 11.30pm–6am; closed Aug;
up to €15. The clubbers' club:
serious about its music, which is
strictly electronic, notably techno. Attracts big-name DJs.

Live music

Au Limonaire

18 Cité Bergère ☎01.45.23.33.33.
Tues–Sat. This tiny, backstreet
place is the perfect intimate and
informal venue for Parisian
chanson, often showcasing committed young singers or zany
music/poetry
/performance acts trying to
catch a break. Dinner before-
hand (traditional, fairly inexpensive and usually quite good)
guarantees a seat for the show at
10pm, otherwise you'll be
crammed up against the bar – if
you can get in at all.

Eglise de la Madeleine

☎ 01.42.50.96.18. A regular venue
for organ recitals and choral
concerts. Tickets €15–23.

Opéra Garnier

☎08.36.69.78.68, 🌐www.opera-de-
paris.fr. The Opéra
Garnier is generally
used for ballets and
smaller-scale opera
productions than those
put on at the Opéra
Bastille. For pro-
gramme and booking
details consult their
website or phone the
box office. Tickets can
cost as little as €6 if
you don't mind being
up in the gods, though
most are in the
€40–60 range.

Beaubourg and Les Halles

One of the city's most recognizable and popular land-marks, the Pompidou Centre, or Beaubourg, as the building is known locally, draws large numbers of visitors to its excellent modern art museum and high-profile exhibitions. Its ground-breaking architecture provoked a storm of controversy on its opening in 1977, but since then it has won over critics and public alike. By contrast, nearby Les Halles, a shopping complex built at around the same time as the Pompidou Centre to replace the old food market that once stood here, has never really endeared itself to the city's inhabitants, though it's worth seeking out some of Les Halles' surviving old bistros and food stalls, which preserve traces of the old market atmosphere.

The Pompidou Centre

ⓦwww.centrepompidou.fr. Built at the heart of one of Paris's oldest districts, the resolutely modern Pompidou Centre is among the twentieth century's most radical buildings. Wanting to move away from the traditional idea of galleries as closed treasure chests to create something more open

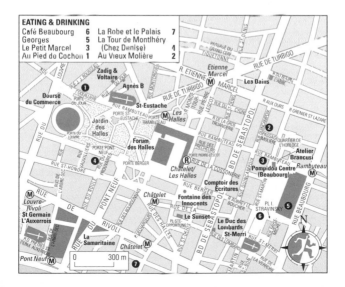

EATING & DRINKING
Café Beaubourg	6	La Robe et le Palais	7
Georges	5	La Tour de Montlhéry	
Le Petit Marcel	3	(Chez Denise)	4
Au Pied du Cochon	1	Au Vieux Molière	2

Beaubourg and Les Halles   PLACES

▲ POMPIDOU CENTRE

and accessible, the architects Renzo Piano and Richard Rogers stripped the "skin" off the building and made all the "bones" visible. The infrastructure was put on the outside: escalator tubes and utility pipes, brightly colour-coded according to their function, climb around the exterior in a crazy snakes-and-ladder fashion. The centre's main draw is its modern art museum and exhibitions, but there are also two cinemas and performance spaces. One of the added treats of visiting the museum is that you get to ascend the transparent escalator on the outside of the building, affording superb views over the city.

Musée National d'Art Moderne

Pompidou Centre. Daily except Tues 11am–9pm. €5.50, audio-guide in English €4.57. The Musée National d'Art Moderne collection is one of the finest of its kind in the world, and is so large that only a fraction of the 50,000 plus works are on show at any one time (they're frequently rotated).

The section covering the years **1905 to 1960** is a near-complete visual essay on the history of modern art: Fauvism, Cubism, Dada, abstract art, Surrealism and abstract expressionism are all well represented. There's a particularly rich collection of Matisses, ranging from early Fauvist works to his late masterpieces – a stand-out is his *Tristesse du Roi*, a moving meditation on old age and memory. Other highlights include a number of Picassos and Braque's early Cubist paintings and a substantial collection of Kandinskys, including his pioneering abstract works *Avec l'arc noir* and *Composition à la tache rouge*. A whole room is devoted to the characteristically colourful paintings of Robert and Sonia Delaunay, while the mood darkens in later rooms with unsettling works by Surrealists Magritte, Dalí and Ernst.

In the **Pop Art** section is Andy Warhol's easily recognizable *Ten Lizes,* in which the actress Elizabeth Taylor sports a Mona Lisa-like smile. Elsewhere Yves Klein prefigures performance art with his *Grande anthropophagie bleue; Hommage à Tennessee Williams*, one in a series of "body prints" in which the artist turned female models into human paintbrushes, covering them in paint to create his artworks.

Established **contemporary artists** you're likely to come across include Claes Oldenburg, Christian Boltanski and Daniel

Buren. Typical of his large *mise-en-scène* installations, Christian Boltanski's *Réserve* is a room hung with lots of musty-smelling secondhand clothes; the effect is oddly oppressive, the absence of the original wearers suggesting death and anonymity. Daniel Buren's works are easy to spot: they all bear his trademark stripes, exactly 8.7cm in width.

Atelier Brancusi

Pompidou Centre. Daily except Tues 2–6pm. Combined ticket with the Musée National d'Art Moderne. The Atelier Brancusi is the reconstructed home and studio of Constantin Brancusi, one of the greatest sculptors of the twentieth century. He bequeathed the contents of his *atelier* to the state on condition that the rooms be arranged exactly as he left them and they provide a fascinating insight into how the artist lived and worked. Studios one and two are crowded with Brancusi's trademark abstract bird and column shapes in highly polished brass and marble, while studios three and four would have been the artist's living quarters.

Quartier Beaubourg

The lively quartier Beaubourg around the Pompidou Centre also offers much in the way of visual art. The colourful, swirling sculptures and fountains in the pool in front of Eglise St Merri on **place Igor Stravinsky**, on the south side of the Pompidou Centre, were created by Jean Tinguely and Niki de St-Phalle; this squirting waterworks pays homage to Stravinsky – each fountain was inspired by one of his compositions (*The Firebird, The Rite of Spring* and so on) but shows scant respect for passers-by.

Numerous commercial galleries take up the contemporary art theme on **rue Quincampoix**, northeast of the Pompidou Centre, the most attractive street in the area: narrow, pedestrianized and lined with fine old *hôtels particuliers*. Also worth exploring is **passage Molière**, an enchanting little alley with some quirky shops, such as Des Mains et des Pieds, where you can get a plaster made of your hand or foot.

▼ PASSAGE MOLIÈRE

▲ HOTEL DE VILLE

Hôtel de Ville

The Hôtel de Ville, the seat of
the city's mayor, is a mansion of
gargantuan proportions in florid
neo-Renaissance style, modelled
pretty much on the previous
building burned down during
the Commune in 1871. The
huge square in front of the Hôtel
de Ville, a notorious guillotine
site during the Revolution,
becomes the location of a popular **ice-skating rink** from
December to February; it's free
and is particularly magical at
night – it's open till midnight on
weekends. You can hire skates for
around €5.

Les Halles

Described by Zola as "*le ventre*
(stomach) *de Paris*", Les Halles
was Paris's main food market for
over eight hundred years until,
despite widespread opposition, it
was moved out to the suburbs in
1969 and replaced by a large
underground shopping and
leisure complex, known as the
Forum des Halles, as well as a
major Métro/RER interchange
(Ⓜ Châtelet-les Halles).

The **Forum des Halles** centre
stretches underground from the
Bourse du Commerce rotunda to
rue Pierre-Lescot and is spread
over four levels. The overground
section comprises aquarium-like
arcades of shops, arranged around
a sunken patio, and landscaped
gardens. The shops are mostly
devoted to high-street fashion,
though there's also a large FNAC
bookshop and the Forum des
Créateurs, an outlet for young
fashion designers.

Little now remains of the old
working-class quarter, but you
can still catch a flavour of the old
market atmosphere in some of
the surrounding bars and bistros
and on pedestrianized **rue
Montorgueil** to the north,
where traditional grocery stalls
and butchers ply their trade
alongside newer arrivals.

St-Eustache

For an antidote to the steel and
glass troglodytism of Les Halles,
head for the soaring vaults of the
beautiful church of St-Eustache.
Built between 1532 and 1637, it's
Gothic in structure, with lofty
naves and graceful flying buttresses, and Renaissance in decoration
– all Corinthian columns,
pilasters and arcades. Molière was
baptized here, and Rameau and
Marivaux are buried here.

▼ LES HALLES

Fontaine des Innocents

The Fontaine des Innocents, a fine Renaissance fountain, decorated with bas-reliefs, is Paris's oldest surviving fountain, dating from 1549. It takes its name from the cemetery that used to occupy this site, the Cimetière des Innocents.

Shops

Agnès B

2, 3, 6, 10, 19 rue du Jour. Mon–Wed, Fri & Sat 10–7, Thurs 10am–9pm. Chic French fashion for men, women and children.

Comptoir des Ecritures

35 rue Quincampoix. Tues–Sat 11am–7pm. A delightful shop entirely devoted to the art of calligraphy, with an extensive collection of paper, pens, brushes and inks.

Pâtisserie Stohrer

51 rue Montorgueil. Daily 7.30am–8pm; closed first two weeks of Aug. Discover what *pain aux raisins* should really taste like at Pâtisserie Stohrer, in business since 1730.

La Samaritaine

75 rue de Rivoli; Mon–Sat 9.30am–7pm, Thurs till 10pm. A splendid Art Nouveau department store, dating back to 1903, recently given something of an upmarket makeover.

Zadig & Voltaire

15 rue du Jour. Mon-Sat 10am-7pm. The women's clothes at this small Parisian chain are pretty and trendy in a relaxed way. In style they're not a million miles from Agnes B, only with a more wayward flair.

Cafés

Café Beaubourg

43 rue St-Merri. Mon–Thurs & Sun 8am–1am, Sat 8am–2am. A seat under the expansive awnings of this stylish café is one of the best places for people-watching on the Pompidou Centre's piazza.

Restaurants

Georges

Pompidou Centre, top floor. Daily except Tues noon–midnight. This cool, ultra-minimalist restaurant commands stunning views over the rooftops of Paris (smoking seats have the best views). The French-Asian fusion cuisine is passable though somewhat overpriced – but then that's not really why you come.

Au Pied de Cochon

6 rue Coquillière. Daily 24hr. A Les Halles institution, this is the place to go for extravagant middle-of-the-night pork chops, oysters and, of course, pigs' trotters.

La Robe et le Palais

13 rue des Lavandières St-Opportune ☎01.45.08.07.41; Mon–Sat noon–2pm & 7.30–11pm. Small, bustling *restaurant à vins* serving traditional cuisine and an excellent selection of wines at reasonable prices.

La Tour de Montlhéry (Chez Denise)

5 rue des Prouvaires ☎01.42.36.21.82; 24hr Mon–Fri; closed mid-July to mid-Aug. An old-style Les Halles bistrot serving substantial food at slightly above average prices; always crowded and smoky.

Au Vieux Molière

Passage Molière, 157 rue Saint-Martin ☎01.42.78.37.87.Tues–Sat noon–2pm & 7.30–11pm, Sun noon–2pm. French chansons playing softly in the background add to the mellow atmosphere of this cosy, candle-lit restaurant serving first-class French cuisine at slightly above average prices.

Bars

Le Petit Marcel

63 rue Rambuteau; Mon–Sat 10am–midnight. Speckled tabletops, mirrors and Art Nouveau tiles, a cracked and faded ceiling and about eight square metres of drinking space. Friendly bar staff and "local" atmosphere.

Live music

Le Duc des Lombards

42 rue des Lombards ☎ 01.42.33.22.88. Daily 7.30pm–3am. €16–19 (depends on when you arrive). A small, unpretentious jazz bar – the place to hear gypsy jazz, blues, ballads and fusion. Performances from 9pm. Drinks around €4.50.

Le Sunset & Le Sunside

60 rue des Lombards ☎01.40.26.46.20. Mon–Sat 9pm–2.30am. €12–20. Two clubs in one: *Le Sunside* on the ground floor features mostly traditional jazz; while the downstairs *Sunset* is a venue for electric and fusion jazz. Attracts some big names.

Clubs

Les Bains

7 rue du Bourg-l'Abbé ☎01.48.87.01.80. Daily midnight–dawn. Mon–Fri €16, Sat & Sun €20. As posey as they come, set in an old Turkish bathhouse with a chill-out area in the old plunge pool. The music is mostly house, hip-hop and garage. Fussy bouncers and expensive drinks.

▲ LE SUNSET

The Marais

Having largely escaped the attentions of Baron Haussmann and unspoiled by modern development, the Marais is one of the most seductive areas of central Paris, full of splendid Renaissance mansions, narrow lanes and buzzing bars and restaurants. Originally little more than a riverside swamp (*marais*), the area was drained and became a magnet for the aristocracy in the early 1600s after the construction of the place des Vosges – or place Royale, as it was then known. This golden age was relatively short-lived, however, for the king took his court to Versailles in the latter part of the seventeenth century and the mansions were left to the trading classes, who were in turn displaced during the Revolution. From then on, the mansions became multi-occupied slum tenements and the streets degenerated into unserviced squalor – hard to believe now that the Marais is one of the most desirable areas in the city.

Gentrification proceeded apace from the 1960s, and the quarter is now known for its sophistication and artsy leanings and for being the neighbourhood of choice for gay Parisians, who are to be credited with bringing both business and style to the area. The city's ancient **Jewish quarter** is also sited here, concentrated on rue des Rosiers.

Prime streets for wandering are rue des Francs Bourgeois, lined with trendy fashion and interior design boutiques, and rue Vieille-du-Temple and rue des Archives, their lively cafés and bars abuzz at all times of day and night. The Marais' animated streets and atmospheric old buildings would be reason enough to visit, but the quarter also boasts an extraordinary concentration of superb museums, not least among them the Musée Picasso, the Carnavalet history museum and the Musée d'Art et d'Histoire du Judaïsme, all set in handsome Renaissance mansions.

Musée d'Art et d'Histoire du Judaïsme

71 rue du Temple ⓦ www.mahj.org. Mon–Fri 11am–6pm, Sun 10am–6pm. €6.10. Housed in the attractively restored Hôtel de Saint-Aignan, the Musée d'Art et d'Histoire du Judaïsme traces the culture and history mainly of the Jews in France. The result is a very comprehensive collection, as educational as it is beautiful.

▼ PLACE DES VOSGES

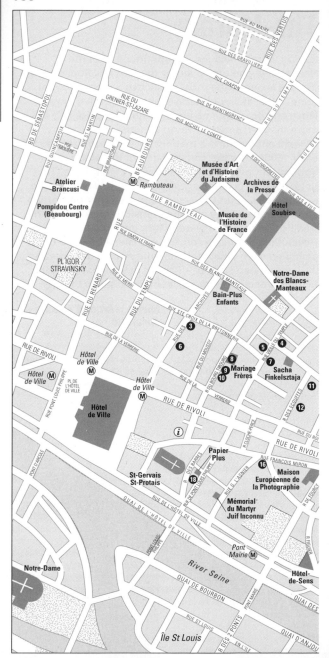

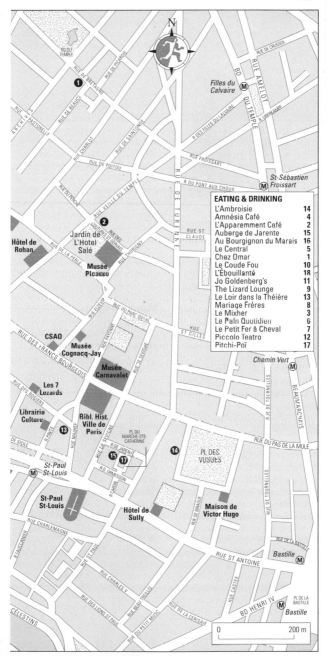

EATING & DRINKING

L'Ambroisie	14
Amnésia Café	4
L'Apparement Café	2
Auberge de Jarente	15
Au Bourgignon du Marais	16
Le Central	5
Chez Omar	1
Le Coude Fou	10
L'Ébouillanté	18
Jo Goldenberg's	11
The Lizard Lounge	9
Le Loir dans la Théière	13
Mariage Fréres	8
Le Mixher	3
Le Pain Quotidien	6
Le Petit Fer à Cheval	7
Piccolo Teatro	12
Pitchi-Poï	17

▲ MUSEE D'ART ET D'HISTOIRE DU JUDAISME

Highlights include a Gothic-style Hanukkah lamp, one of the very few French Jewish artefacts to survive from the period before the expulsion of the Jews from France in 1394; an Italian gilded circumcision chair from the seventeenth century; and a completely intact late-nine-teenth-century Austrian *Sukkah*, a temporary dwelling for the celebration of the harvest.

The museum also holds the Dreyfus archives, with one room devoted to the notorious Dreyfus affair.

The last few rooms contain a significant collection of paintings and sculpture by Jewish artists – Marc Chagall, Samuel Hirszenberg, Chaïm Soutine and Jacques Lipchitz – who came to live in Paris at the beginning of the twentieth century.

The only reference to the Holocaust is an installation by contemporary artist Christian Boltanski: its very understatement has a powerful impact.

Hôtel Soubise

60 rue des Francs-Bourgeois. Mon & Wed–Fri 10am–12.30pm & 2–5.30pm, Sat & Sun 2–5.30pm. €3. The entire block from rue des Quatre Fils and rue des Archives, and from rue Vieille-du-Temple to rue des Francs-Bourgeois, was once filled by a magnificent early eighteenth-century palace complex. Only half remains today, but it is utterly splendid, especially the grand colonnaded courtyard of the Hôtel Soubise, with its vestigial fourteenth-century towers on rue des Quatre Fils. Restoration works on the hôtel's fabulous Rococo decor will keep visitors out for all of 2004 and part of 2005, but meanwhile you can see plenty of sumptuous interiors at the adjacent Hôtel de Rohan, notably the charming, Chinese-inspired Cabinet des Singes, whose walls are painted with monkeys acting out various aristocratic scenes.

Musée Picasso

5 rue de Thorigny. Daily except Tues 9.30am–6pm, Thurs till 8pm, March & April till 5.30pm. €5.50, Sun €4. Behind the elegant classical facade of the seventeenth-century Hôtel Salé lies the Musée Picasso. It's the largest

▼ HOTEL SOUBISE

collection of Picassos anywhere, representing almost all the major periods of the artist's life from 1905 onwards. Many of the works were owned by Picasso and on his death in 1973 were seized by the state in lieu of taxes owed. The result is an unedited body of work, which, although perhaps not among the most recognizable of Picasso's masterpieces, provides a sense of the artist's development and an insight into the person behind the myth.

Some of the most engaging works on display are his more personal ones – those depicting his wives, lovers and children. Portraits of his lovers, Dora Maar and Marie-Thérèse, exhibited side by side in room 13, show how the two women inspired Picasso in very different ways: they strike the same pose, but Dora Maar is painted with strong lines and vibrant colours, suggesting a passionate, vivacious personality, while Marie-Thérèse's muted colours and soft contours convey serenity and peace.

The museum also holds a substantial number of Picasso's engravings, ceramics and sculpture, reflecting the remarkable ease with which the artist moved from one medium to another. Some of the most arresting sculptures (room 17) are those he created from recycled household objects, such as the endearing *La Chèvre (Goat)*, whose stomach is made from a basket, and the *Tête de taureau (Bull's head)*, an ingenious pairing of a bicycle seat and handlebars.

Musée Cognacq-Jay

8 rue Elzévir. Tues–Sun 10am–5.40pm. Free. The compact Musée Cognacq Jay occupies the fine Hôtel Donon. The Cognacq-Jay family built up the Samaritaine department store (see p.103) and were noted philanthropists and lovers of European art. Their collection of eighteenth-century pieces on show includes works by Canaletto, Fragonard, Rubens and Rembrandt, as well as an exquisite still life by Chardin, displayed in beautifully carved wood-panelled rooms filled with Sèvres porcelain and Louis XV furniture.

Musée Carnavalet

23 rue de Sévigné. Tues–Sun 10am–6pm. Free. The fascinating Musée Carnavalet charts the history of Paris from its origins up to the *belle époque* through an extraordinary collection of paintings, sculptures, decorative arts and archeological finds – spread over 140 rooms. The museum's setting in two beautiful Renaissance mansions, Hôtel Carnavalet and Hôtel Le Peletier, surrounded by attractive gardens, is worth a visit in itself.

Among the highlights on the **ground floor**, devoted largely to the early history of Paris, is the recently renovated orangery housing a significant collection of Neolithic finds, including a number of wooden pirogues unearthed during the redevelopment of the Bercy riverside area in the 1990s.

▲ MUSEE CARNAVALET

On the **first floor**, decorative arts feature strongly, with numerous re-created salons and boudoirs full of richly sculpted wood panelling and tapestries from the time of Louis XII to Louis XVI, rescued from buildings that had to be destroyed for Haussmann's boulevards. Room 21 is devoted to the famous letter-writer Madame de Sévigné, who lived in the Carnavalet mansion and wrote a series of letters to her daughter, which vividly portray her privileged lifestyle under the reign of Louis XIV. Rooms 128 to 148 are largely devoted to the *belle époque*, evoked through numerous paintings of the period and some wonderful Art Nouveau interiors, most stunning of which is a jewellery shop, with its peacock-green decor and swirly motifs, designed by Alphonse Mucha and reassembled here in its entirety. Also well preserved is José-Maria Sert's Art Deco ballroom, with its extravagant gold-leaf decor and grand-scale paintings, including one of the Queen of Sheba with a train of elephants. Nearby is a section on

literary life at the beginning of the twentieth century, including a reconstruction of Proust's cork-lined bedroom (room 147).

The **second floor** has rooms full of mementoes of the French Revolution: original declarations of the Rights of Man and the Citizen, glorious models of the guillotine, crockery with revolutionary slogans and even execution orders to make you shed a tear for the royalists as well.

The Jewish quarter: rue des Rosiers

Crammed with kosher food shops, delicatessens, restaurants and Hebrew bookstores, the narrow, bustling rue des Rosiers has been the heart of the city's Jewish quarter ever since the twelfth century, and remains so, despite incursions by trendy bars and clothes shops. There's also a distinctly Mediterranean flavour to the quarter, as seen in the many falafel stalls, testimony to the influence of the North African Sephardim, who, since the end of World War II, have sought refuge here from the uncertainties of life in the former French colonies.

Place des Vosges

A vast square of symmetrical pink
brick and stone mansions built
over arcades, the place des Vosges
is a masterpiece of aristocratic
elegance and the first example of
planned development in the history of Paris. It was built by
Henri IV and inaugurated in
1612 for the wedding of Louis
XIII and Anne of Austria; Louis's
statue – or, rather, a replica of it –
stands hidden by chestnut trees in
the middle of the grass and gravel
gardens at the square's centre.

Through all the vicissitudes of
history, the *place* has never lost its
cachet as a smart address. Today,
well-heeled Parisians pause in
the arcades at art, antique and
fashion shops, and lunch alfresco
in the restaurants while buskers
play classical music. The garden is
the only green space of any size
in the locality – unusually for
Paris, you're allowed to sprawl on
the grass.

Maison de Victor Hugo

Tues–Sun 10am–6pm, closed hols. Free.
Among the many celebrities who
made their homes in place des
Vosges was Victor Hugo; his
house, at no. 6, where he wrote
much of *Les Misérables*, is now a
museum, the Maison de Victor
Hugo. Hugo was extraordinarily
multi-talented: as well as being a
prolific writer, he enjoyed sketch-
ing and designed his own furniture. Nearly five hundred of his
ink drawings are on display, and a
richly decorated Chinese-style
dining room that he designed for
his house in Guernsey is recreat-
ed here in all its splendour.

Hôtel de Sully

62 rue St-Antoine. Tues–Sun
10am–6.30pm. €4.
The exquisite Renaissance
Hôtel de Sully is home to temporary photographic exhibitions, usually with social, historical or anthropological themes,
mounted by the **Mission du
Patrimoine Photographique**.
The mansion's formal garden,
with its orangery and park
benches, makes for a peaceful
rest-stop.

The Quartier St-Paul-St-Gervais

The southern section of the
Marais, below rues de Rivoli
and St-Antoine, harbours some
of Paris's most atmospheric
streets: rue Cloche-Perce with
its crooked steps and lanterns;
rue François-Miron lined with
tottering medieval timbered
houses; and cobbled rue des
Barres, filled with the scent of
roses from nearby gardens and
sometimes the waft of incense
from the church of St-Gervais-
St-Protais, a late Gothic construction that looks somewhat
battered on the outside owing
to a direct hit from a shell fired
from a Big Bertha howitzer in
1918. Its interior contains some
lovely stained glass, carved mis-
ericords and a seventeenth-
century organ – Paris's oldest.

▼ JEWISH QUARTER DELI

Maison Européenne de la Photographie

4 rue de Fourcy. Wed–Sun 11am–8pm.
€5, free Wed after 5pm. A gorgeous
Marais mansion, the early eighteenth-century Hôtel Hénault de
Cantobre, has been turned into a
vast and serene space dedicated to
the art of contemporary photography. Temporary shows combine
with a revolving exhibition of the
Maison's permanent collection;
young photographers and news
photographers get a look-in, as
well as artists using photography
in multimedia creations or installation art. A library and *videothèque*
can be freely consulted, and
there's a stylish café designed by
architect Nestor Perkal.

Shops

Archives de la Presse

51 rue des Archives. Mon–Sat
10.30am–7pm. A fascinating shop
trading in old French newspapers and magazines. The
window always has a display of
outdated newspapers corre-
sponding to the current month,
and there are piles upon piles
of old magazines inside.

Bain – Plus Enfants

23 rue des Blancs Manteaux. Tues–Sat
11am–7.30pm. Aimed at kids up to
12 years old, this stylish shop has an
irresistible range of bed and bath
items: chic pyjamas, hooded robes,
fluffy towels and cuddly bears.

CSAO (Compagnie du Sénégal et de l'Afrique de l'Ouest)

1 & 3 rue Elzévir. Mon–Sat 11am–7pm,
Sun 2–7pm. Fairly traded crafts
and artwork from West Africa,
including Malian cotton scarves
in rich, earthy tones and painted
glass from Senegal.

▲ MARAIS CHIC

Librairie Culture

17 bis rue Pavée. Mon–Sat 10.30–7pm.
A real Aladdin's cave, spread over
three floors, with books piled up
everywhere you look – mostly
secondhand and returns, with
some good deals on art titles.

Mariage Frères

30 rue du Bourg-Tibourg. Shop daily
10.30am–7.30pm. café daily
noon–7pm. Hundreds of teas,
neatly packed in tins, line the
floor-to-ceiling shelves of this
100-year-old tea emporium.
There's also a classy, neo-colo-
nial-style *salon de thé* on the
ground floor.

Papier Plus

9 rue du Pont-Louis-Philippe.
Mon–Sat noon–7pm. Fine-quality,
colourful stationery, including
notebooks, photo albums and
artists' portfolios.

Sacha Finkelsztajn

27 rue des Rosiers. Wed–Mon
10am–2pm & 3–7pm; closed Aug.
Marvellous Jewish deli for take-
away snacks and goodies: East
European breads, apple strudel,
gefilte fish, aubergine purée, tara-
ma, *blinis* and *borsch*.

Cafés

Amnésia Café

42 rue Vieille-du-Temple. Daily 10am–2am. Forget your troubles over drinks and sandwiches in the alluring ambience of this low-lit, spacious café. Popular brunch served from noon to 5pm. Gets pretty wild at night; primarily gay, but straight-friendly.

L'Apparemment Café

18 rue des Coutures-St-Gervais. Mon–Fri noon–2am, Sat 4pm–2am, Sun 12.30pm–midnight. A chic but cosy café resembling a series of comfortable sitting rooms, with quiet corners and deep sofas. Popular Sunday brunch until 4pm.

L'Ebouillanté

6 rue des Barres. Tues–Sun noon–10pm, till 9pm in winter. A two-floor café that spills onto the picturesque rue des Barres in nice weather. There's an extensive choice of drinks, from delicious homemade hot chocolate to iced fruit cocktails, and snacks, including Tunisian crêpes.

Le Loir dans la Théière

3 rue des Rosiers. Sun–Thurs 11am–7pm, Fri & Sat 10am–7pm. A convivial and trendy *salon de thé*, where you can sink into battered sofas and pit yourself against challenging portions of scrummy, homemade cakes.

L'Open Café

17 rue des Archives ☎01.42.72.26.18 Daily 11am–2am. A popular gay café, heaving at night with a hip club crowd.

Maison Européenne de la Photographie Café

4 rue de Fourcy. Thurs–Sun 11am–7pm, Wed 11am–5pm. A stylish café in the atmospheric, seventeenth-century Hôtel Hénault de Cantobre.

Mariage Frères

30 rue du Bourg Tibourg. Daily noon–7pm. A classy *salon de thé* on the ground floor of this tea emporium, decorated in neo-colonial style with rattan furniture.

Le Pain Quotidien

18 rue des Archives. Daily 8am–7pm. A trendy café-bakery where you

▼ MARIAGE FRERES TEA SHOP

have the option of rubbing shoulders with fellow diners at a long, communal *table d'hôte*. It specializes in hearty salads, *tartines* (open sandwiches) and excellent breads.

Bars

Le Central

33 rue Vieille-du-Temple. Mon–Thurs 4pm–2am. The oldest gay local in the Marais. Small, friendly and always crowded with locals and tourists.

The Lizard Lounge

18 rue du Bourg-Tibourg. Daily noon–2am. A loud, lively, stone-walled bar on two levels; American-run and popular with young expats. Especially busy for Sunday brunch, featuring Bloody Marys.

Le Mixer

23 rue Sainte-Croix-de-la-Bretonnerie. Daily 5pm–2am. A popular and crowded Marais bar, raising the pulse of gay and straight pre-clubbers with its pounding techno and house soundtrack.

Le Petit Fer à Cheval

30 rue Vieille-du-Temple. Mon–Fri 9am–2am, Sat & Sun 11am–2am; food served noon–midnight. A very attractive small *bistrot*-bar with original *fin-de-siècle* decor. You can snack on sandwiches or light meals in the little back room furnished with old wooden Métro seats.

Restaurants

L'Ambroisie

9 place des Vosges ☎01.42.78.51.45. Tues–Sat noon–2pm & 7–10.15pm;

closed Aug. Scoring 19 out of 20 in the gourmet's bible *Gault et Millau*, *L'Ambroisie* offers exquisite food in a magnificent dining room hung with tapestries. Reckon on upwards of €200 and book well in advance.

Auberge de Jarente

7 rue Jarente ☎01.42.77.49.35. Tues–Sat noon–2.30pm & 7.30–10.30pm; closed Aug. This inexpensive and friendly Basque restaurant serves up first-class food – *cassoulet*, hare stew, *magret de canard*, and *pipérade*.

Au Bourgignon du Marais

52 rue François Miron ☎01.48.87.15.40. Mon–Fri noon–3pm & 8–11pm; closed two weeks in Aug. A warm, relaxed restaurant with tables outside in summer, serving excellent Burgundian cuisine with carefully selected wines to match. Prices slightly above average. Booking advised.

Le Coude Fou

12 rue du Bourg-Tibourg ☎01.42.77.15.16. Daily noon–2.45pm & 7.30–midnight. A popular, reasonably priced, laid-back wine *bistro*, with wooden beams and

▼ RUE VIEILLE-DU-TEMPLE

▲ LE PETIT FER A CHEVAL CAFE

brightly painted murals.
Booking advisable at weekends.

Jo Goldenberg's

7 rue des Rosiers. Daily noon–2pm &
7.30pm–1.30am. Dating back to
the 1920s, this is the best
known Jewish restaurant in the
capital, serving decent *borsch, blinis, zakouski* and *apfel strudel,* and
sometimes there's live music,
often a violin and guitar duo
playing jazz favourites. Prices
above average.

Piccolo Teatro

6 rue des Ecouffes ☎01.42.72.17.79.
Tues–Sun noon–3pm & 7.15–11pm;
closed Aug. A great, inexpensive
vegetarian restaurant with low
lighting, stone walls and wooden
beams. The speciality is *gratins,*
with poetic names such as
douceur et tendresse (spinach,
mint, mozzarella and Gruyère).
Best to book at weekends.

Pitchi-Poï

7 rue Caron, cnr place du Marché-Ste-
Catherine ☎01.42.77.46.15. Daily
10am–midnight. A homely, moderately priced restaurant with outdoor seating on one of the
Marais' most attractive squares.
The cuisine revolves around
central European/Jewish dishes
and you can sample a range of
Polish flavoured vodkas – the
honey one goes down a treat.

Chez Omar

47 Rue de Bretagne, ☎01.42.72.36.26.
Daily except Sun lunch noon–2.30pm
& 7–11.30pm; no credit cards. A very
popular, inexpensive North
African couscous restaurant in a
nice old brasserie set with mirrors, attracting a young crowd.

Live music

Les 7 Lézards

10 rue des Rosiers ☎01.48.87.08.97,
🌐www.7lezards.com. Wed–Sat
7.15pm–2am; €10–16. A cosy and
intimate jazz club, attracting
international and local acts.
Also hosts the odd world music
gig, and there's a decent restaurant, too.

The Quartier Latin

The **Quartier Latin** has been associated with students ever since the **Sorbonne** was established back in the thirteenth century. The odd name derives from the Latin spoken at the medieval university, which perched on the slopes of the **Montagne Ste-Geneviève**. Many colleges remain in the area to this day, along with some fascinating vestiges of the medieval city, such as the Gothic church of **St-Séverin** and the Renaissance **Hôtel de Cluny**, site of the national museum of the Middle Ages. Some of the quarter's student chic may have worn thin in recent years – notably around the now too-famous **place St-Michel** – and high rents may have pushed scholars and artists out of their garrets, but the quarter's cafés, restaurants and arty cinemas are still packed with young people, making this one of the most relaxed areas of Paris for going out.

The Huchette quarter

The touristy bustle is at its worst around rue de la Huchette, just east of the place St-Michel, but look beyond the cheap bars and over-priced Greek seafood-and-disco tavernas and you'll find some evocative remnants of medieval Paris. Connecting rue de la Huchette to the riverside is the incredibly narrow rue du Chat-qui-Pêche, a tiny slice of how Paris used to look before Baron Haussmann flattened the old alleys to make room for his wide boulevards.

The mainly fifteenth-century church of St-Séverin is one of the city's more intense churches. Its Flamboyant choir rests on a spiralling central pillar – a virtuoso piece of stonework– and its windows are filled with edgy stained glass by the modern French painter Jean Bazaine. The flame-like carving that gave the Flamboyant (blazing) style its name flickers in the window arch above the

entrance, while inside, the first three pillars of the nave betray the earlier, thirteenth-century origins of the church.

The riverbank

The riverbank *quais* east of place St-Michel are ideal for wandering, and you can browse among the books, postcards,

▼ CHAPELLE STE-URSULE SORBONNE

▲ FLAMBOYANT VAULT AT ST-SEVERIN

a bold slice of glass and steel that betrays Nouvel's obsession with light – its rectangular southern façade comprises thousands of tiny light-sensitive shutters that modulate the light levels inside while simultaneously mimicking a *moucharabiyah* (traditional Arab latticework balcony).

Inside, it's a cultural centre designed to further national understanding of the Arab world. There are good temporary exhibitions on Arab and Islamic art and culture, and regular films and concerts, often featuring leading performers from the Arab world. But the heart of the institute is its sleek **museum**, which traces the evolution of Islamic art and civilization. Brass celestial globes, astrolabes, compasses and sundials illustrate cutting-edge Arab medieval science, while exquisitely crafted ceramics, metalwork and carpets from all over the Muslim world cover the artistic side. Up on the ninth floor, the terrace has brilliant views over the Seine towards the apse of Notre-Dame.

prints and assorted goods on sale from the *bouquinistes*, who display their wares in green, padlocked boxes hooked onto the parapet. There are wonderful views of Notre-Dame across the Seine, especially from **square Viviani** – a welcome patch of grass with an ancient, listing tree reputed to be Paris's oldest, a false acacia brought over from Guyana in 1680. The mutilated church behind is **St-Julien-le-Pauvre** (daily 9.30am–12.30pm & 3–6.30pm), which used to be the venue for university assemblies until rumbustious students tore it apart in 1524. For the most dramatic view of Notre-Dame of all, walk along the riverbank as far as the tip of the Ile St-Louis and the Pont de Sully.

Institut du Monde Arabe

Tues–Sun 10am–6pm; museum €4. ⓦwww.imarabe.org. Many visitors come to the Institut du Monde Arabe (IMA) just to admire its stunning design – the work of Paris's hippest architect, Jean Nouvel. On the outside, the IMA is

▼ INSTITUT DU MONDE ARABE

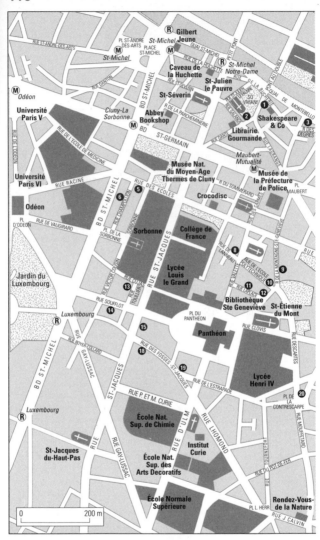

The Musée National du Moyen Age

Entrance at 6 place Paul-Painlevé. Mon & Wed–Sun 9.15am–5.45pm. €5.50, €4 on Sun. Concerts Fri 12.30pm & Sat 4pm. ⊛www.musee-moyenage.fr. The Hôtel de Cluny, an attrac-

tive sixteenth-century mansion built by the abbots of the powerful Cluny monastery as their Paris pied-à-terre, now houses the richly rewarding Musée National du Moyen Age. The museum is an amazing ragbag of

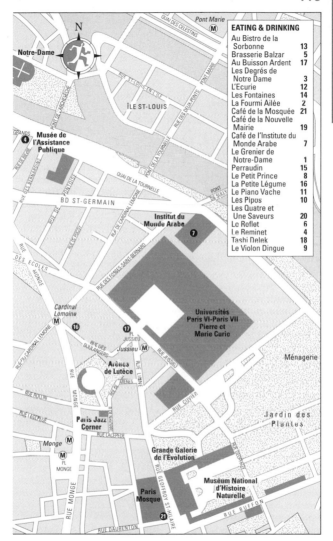

EATING & DRINKING

Au Bistro de la Sorbonne	13
Brasserie Balzar	5
Au Buisson Ardent	17
Les Degrés de Notre Dame	3
L'Ecurie	12
Les Fontaines	14
La Fourmi Ailée	2
Café de la Mosquée	21
Café de la Nouvelle Mairie	19
Café de l'Institute du Monde Arabe	7
Le Grenier de Notre-Dame	1
Perraudin	15
Le Petit Prince	8
La Petite Légume	16
Le Piano Vache	11
Les Pipos	10
Les Quatre et Une Saveurs	20
Le Roflet	6
Le Reminet	4
Tashi Delek	18
Le Violon Dingue	9

tapestries, carved choir stalls, altarpieces, ivories, stained glass, illuminated Books of Hours, games, brassware and all manner of precious *objets d'art*. The greatest wonder of the collection is the exquisitely executed late fifteenth-century tapestry series known as the *Lady with the Unicorn*, displayed in a specially darkened, chapel-like chamber on the first floor. Even if you don't immediately grasp the tapestries' allegorical

▲ MUSEE DU MOYEN AGE ENTRANCE

meaning – they represent the five senses – it's hard not to be blown away by the sheer wealth of detail and richness of colour. The meaning of the sixth and final tapestry is something of a mystery: the scene is of a woman putting away her necklace into a jewellery box held out by her servant, captioned with the words *A Mon Seul Désir* ("To My Only Desire").

The building itself is part of the attraction of the visit: some rooms are decorated in the original style, and the Flamboyant Gothic chapel preserves its remarkable vault splaying out from a central pillar. You can also explore the remains of Paris's third-century Roman baths, the **Thermes de Cluny**, whose characteristic rounded arches and stripey brickwork can also be seen from the boulevard St-Michel.

It's worth timing your visit to coincide with one of the excellent concerts of medieval music, often held inside the museum.

Place de la Sorbonne

The traffic-free place de la Sorbonne is a great place to sit back and enjoy the Quartier Latin atmosphere, with its lime trees, fountains, cafés and book-toting students. Frowning over it, however, are the high walls of the **Sorbonne**, once the most important of the medieval colleges huddled on the top of the Montagne Ste-Geneviève and more recently a flashpoint in the 1968 student riots. The frontage is dominated by the Chapelle Ste-Ursule, built in the 1640s by the great Cardinal Richelieu, whose tomb it contains. A building of enormous influence in Paris for its unabashed emulation of the Roman Counter-Reformation style, it also helped establish a trend for domes, many more of which mushroomed over the city's skyline in the latter part of the seventeenth century.

The Panthéon

Daily: April–Sept 10am–6.30pm; Oct–March 10am–6pm. €7.
Crowning the very top of the Montagne Ste-Geneviève, the largest and most visible of Paris's

▼ PANTHEON

121

over a twenty-four-hour period, it was in fact the earth beneath it turning.

St-Etienne-du-Mont

The remains of two seventeenth-century literary giants, Pascal and Racine, lie in the church of St-Etienne-du-Mont, alongside a few relics of Paris's early patron, Ste-Geneviève, housed in a luxuriously appointed chapel. The main attraction, however, is the fabulously airy interior, formed of a Flamboyant Gothic choir joined to a Renaissance nave, the two parts linked by a sinuous catwalk that runs right round the interior, arching across the width of the nave in the form of a carved rood screen – an extremely rare survival, as most French screens fell victim to Protestant iconoclasts, reformers or revolutionaries.

Contrescarpe and rue Mouffetard

Encircled by cafés, tiny place de la Contrescarpe is the focal point for the student nightlife of the Quartier Latin, and it's a

domes graces the bulky Panthéon, Louis XV's thank-you to Sainte Geneviève, patron saint of Paris, for curing him of illness. The building was completed only in 1789, whereupon the Revolution promptly transformed it into a mausoleum, emblazoning the front with the words "*Aux grands hommes la patrie reconnaissante*" ("The nation honours its great men") underneath the pediment of the giant portico. Down in the vast, barrel-vaulted crypt, you can visit the tombs of French cultural giants such as Voltaire, Hugo and Zola, along with more recent arrivals Marie Curie – the only woman – and Alexandre Dumas, author of *The Three Musketeers*.

In the nave, you can also see a working model of Foucault's Pendulum swinging from the dome. French physicist Léon Foucault devised the experiment, conducted here in 1851, to demonstrate that while the pendulum appeared to rotate

▼ RUE MOUFFETARD MARKET STALL

pleasant spot to have a drink or a coffee during the day.

Stretching downhill from the square, the narrow, medieval rue Mouffetard – rue Mouff' to locals – may not be the quintessentially Parisian market street it once was but it still offers an honest local ambience, lined with clothes and shoe shops, a giant health food centre, and lots of unpretentious bars and restaurants. The lower half of the street maintains a few grocers' stalls, butcheries and speciality cheese shops, with a fruit-and-veg market on Tuesday and Saturday mornings.

The Paris mosque

Entrance on rue Daubenton, at southeast corner of the mosque. Daily except Fri & Muslim hols 9am–noon & 2–6pm. €3. Even in this quiet, residential area, the Paris mosque feels like an oasis of serenity behind its high, crenellated walls. You can walk in the sunken garden and patios with their polychrome tiles and carved ceilings, but non-Muslims are asked not to enter the prayer room – though no one seems to mind if you watch from a discreet distance during prayers.

The Paris mosque's hammam

39 rue Geoffrey-St-Hilaire. Women Mon, Wed, Thurs & Sat 10am–9pm, Fri 2–9pm. Men Tues 2–9pm, Sun 10am–9pm. Times may vary, check in advance. €15, towels extra. The excellent hammam in the Paris mosque, entered via the gate in the southeast corner, is one of the most atmospheric baths in the city, with its vaulted cooling-off room and marble-lined steam chamber. It's usually quiet inside, the clients focused on washing and simply relaxing, so the atmosphere shouldn't feel intimidating, even if you've

never taken a public bath before. You can also have a reasonably priced massage and *gommage* – a kind of rubber-gloved rub-down for exfoliating. Afterwards, slip into the lovely, gardened **tearoom** (open to all, even if you haven't used the hammam) for mint tea and sweet pastries.

Jardin des Plantes

Entrances at the corner of rues Geoffroy-St-Hilaire and Buffon and at three points along rue Cuvier. Daily: summer 7.30am–8pm; winter 7.30am–dusk. The magnificent, varied floral beds of the Jardin des Plantes were founded as a medicinal herb garden in 1626 and gradually evolved into Paris's botanical gardens, with hothouses, shady avenues of trees, lawns, a brace of museums and a zoo.

The gardens make a pleasant place to while away the middle of a day. Near the rue Cuvier entrance stands a fine cedar of Lebanon, planted in 1734 and raised from seed sent over from the Botanical Gardens in Oxford. There's also a slice of an American sequoia more than 2000 years old, with the birth of Christ and other historical events marked on its rings. On a cold day there's no better place to warm up than the hot and humid winter garden, a greenhouse filled with palms, cacti and chattering birds.

Grande Galerie de l'Evolution

Muséum National d'Histoire Naturelle, Jardin des Plantes. ⊛www.mnhn.fr/evolution. Mon & Wed–Sun 10am–6pm, Thurs 10am–10pm. €7. Part of the Muséum National d'Histoire Naturelle, and by far its most impressive section, is the Grande Galerie de l'Evolution. It occupies the

nineteenth-century Galerie de Zoologie, an enormous, dark space surrounded by tier upon tier of glass and iron balconies, dramatically lit by glowing spotlights. The museum tells the story of evolution and the relations between human beings and nature with the aid of a huge cast of life-size animals that parade across the central space. The wow-factor may initially grab children's attention, but you'll have to look out for the translation placards to make the most of the visit.

The Ménagerie

Northeast corner of the Jardin des Plantes. Summer Mon–Sat 9am–6pm, Sun 9am–6.30pm; winter Mon–Sat 9am–5pm, Sun 9am–5.30pm. €6. The Ménagerie is France's oldest zoo – and feels it. The iron cages of the big cats' *fauverie*, the stinky vivarium and the glazed-in primate house are distinctly old-fashioned, though most of the rest of the zoo is pleasantly park-like, given over to deer, antelope, goats, buffaloes and other marvellous beasts that seem happy enough in their outdoor enclosures.

Arènes de Lutèce

The Arènes de Lutèce is an unexpected and peaceful backwater hidden from the streets. Once a Roman amphitheatre for ten thousand, it is now the only structure from that period left in Paris besides the Gallo-Roman baths (see p.120). A few ghostly rows of stone seats now look down on boules players, while benches, gardens and a kids' playground stand behind.

Shops

Abbey Bookshop/La Librairie Canadienne

29 rue de la Parcheminerie. Mon–Sat 10am–7pm. A Canadian bookshop with lots of secondhand British and North American fiction, plus knowledgeable and helpful staff – and free coffee.

Crocodisc

40–42 rue des Ecoles. Tues–Sat 11am–7pm. Folk, Oriental, Afro-Antillais, raï, funk, reggae, salsa, hip-hop, soul and country music, both new and secondhand, at some of the best prices in town.

▲ GIBERT JEUNE

Gibert Jeune

10 place St-Michel & 27 quai St-Michel. Mon–Sat 10am–7pm. The biggest of the Quartier Latin student/academic bookshops with a vast selection of French books. There's a fair English-language and discounted selection at Gibert Joseph, 26 bd St-Michel. An institution.

Librairie Gourmande

4 rue Dante. Daily 10am–7pm. The very last word in books on cookery and food in general, with a decent English-language selection.

Paris Jazz Corner

5 & 7 rue Navarre. Mon–Sat noon–8pm. Great collection of jazz and blues, with lots of secondhand vinyl. Worth visiting for the dustily dedicated atmosphere of the shop alone, which faces the Arènes de Lutèce.

Rendez-Vous de la Nature

96 rue Mouffetard. Tues–Sat 9.30am–7.30pm, Sun 9.30am–1pm.

One of the city's most comprehensive health-food stores, with everything from organic produce to herbal teas.

Shakespeare & Co

37 rue de la Bûcherie. Daily noon–midnight. A cosy, famous literary haunt, American-run – by the gransdon of Walt Whitman – with the biggest selection of secondhand English books in town. Also holds poetry readings and the like.

Cafés

Café de la Mosquée

39 rue Geoffroy-St-Hilaire. Daily 9am–11pm. Drink mint tea and eat sweet cakes beside a fountain and assorted fig trees in the courtyard of this Paris mosque – a delightful haven of calm. The salon has a beautiful Arabic interior, while full meals are served in the adjoining restaurant.

La Fourmi Ailée

8 rue du Fouarre, on sq Viviani. Daily noon–midnight. Simple, light fare is served in this former bookshop, now transformed into a relaxed *salon de thé*. The high ceiling, painted with a lovely mural, and a book-filled wall contribute to the atmosphere. Serves inexpensive *plats du jour*.

Café de l'Institut du Monde Arabe

Institut du Monde Arabe. Tues–Sun 10am–6pm. Amazing rooftop café-restaurant where you can drink mint tea and nibble on cakes in the sunshine. Inside the building, the self-service cafeteria *Moucharabiyah* offers a good plate of lunchtime couscous and the chance to marvel at the aperture action of the windows.

Café de la Nouvelle Mairie

19 rue des Fossés-St-Jacques. Mon, Wed & Fri 9am–10pm, Tues & Thurs 9am–11pm. Sleek café-wine bar with a relaxed feel generated by its older, university-based clientele. Serves good, reasonably priced food such as *curry*

d'agneau, linguine and salads, and you can drink at the outside tables on sunny days.

Le Reflet

6 rue Champollion. Daily 10am–2am. This artsy cinema café has a strong flavour of the *nouvelle vague*, with its scruffy black paint scheme, lights rigged up on a gantry overhead and rickety tables packed with arty film-goers and chess players. Good steaks, quiches, salads and the like from a short list of blackboard specials.

Restaurants

Au Bistro de la Sorbonne

4 rue Toullier ☎01.43.54.41.49. Daily noon–2.30pm & 7–11pm. Traditional French and delicious North African food served at reasonable prices to a crowd of locals and students. The muralled interior is attractively bright.

Brasserie Balzar

49 rue des Ecoles ☎01.43.54.13.67. Daily 8am–11.30pm. This mirrored,

▼ SHAKESPEARE & CO

high-ceilinged brasserie is festooned with pot plants in the classic style. Earlier on, the atmosphere can be quite touristy, but if you choose to eat late it becomes almost intimidatingly Parisian – which about fits the decor and the menu. Prices are fairly expensive for a traditional brasserie, but you won't break the bank.

Au Buisson Ardent

25 rue Jussieu ☎ 01.43.54.93.02. Mon–Fri 12.30–2.30pm & 7.30–10pm, Sat 7.30–10pm; closed two weeks in Aug. Copious helpings of inventive, first-class cooking served in a warm-coloured, pleasantly traditional dining room. Prices are moderate. Reservations recommended.

Les Degrés de Notre Dame

10 rue des Grands Degrés ☎ 01.55.42.88.88. Mon–Sat noon–2.30pm & 7.30–10.30pm. This reliable, informal little restaurant serves substantial and very inexpensive French food. Good for a cosy lunch-stop.

L'Ecurie

58 rue de la Montagne Ste-Geneviève, cnr rue Laplace. Mon–Sat noon–3pm & 7pm–midnight, Sun 7pm–midnight. Shoehorned into a former stables on a particularly lovely corner of the Montagne Ste-Geneviève, this small, family-run restaurant is bustling and very lovable. Expect well-cooked, inexpensive meat dishes served without flourishes.

Les Fontaines

9 rue Soufflot. Mon–Sat noon–3pm & 7.30–10.30pm. The brasserie decor looks unpromising from the outside, but the welcome inside this family-owned place is warm and genuine, and the cooking is in the same spirit,

with honest French meat and fish dishes, or game in season, all at reasonable prices.

Le Grenier de Notre-Dame

18 rue de la Bûcherie ☎ 01.43.29.98.29. Mon–Sat noon–3pm & 7.30–10.30pm. Vegetarians' opinions are divided: some love this tiny, candle-lit place; others find it cramped and the atmosphere too eagerly created. Dishes are substantial and fairly inexpensive, including traditional French fare made with tofu and unreconstructed vegetarian classics such as cauliflower cheese.

Perraudin

157 rue St-Jacques ☎ 01.46.33.15.75. Mon–Fri noon–2pm & 7.30–10.15pm; closed last fortnight in Aug. One of the classic *bistrots* of the Left Bank. The atmosphere is thick with Parisian chatter floating above the brightly lit, packed-in tables. Solid cooking, with moderately priced menus. No reservations.

Le Petit Prince

12 rue Lanneau ☎ 01.43.54.77.26. Mon–Thurs & Sun 7.30pm–midnight, Fri & Sat 7.30pm–12.30am. *The Little Prince* serves moderately priced, classic French food with occasionally inventive combinations that can be hit and miss. Most of the tables are hidden away at the cosy end of the restaurant, where there's often a good-time atmosphere created by a fairly camp crowd.

La Petite Légume

36 rue Boulangers ☎ 01.40.46.06.85. Mon–Sat noon–2.30pm & 7.30–10pm. A health-food grocery that doubles as a vegetarian restaurant and tearoom, serving homely, inexpensive organic *plats*, along with fresh-tasting organic Loire wines.

Les Quatre et Une Saveurs

72 rue du Cardinal-Lemoine
☎01.43.26.88.80. Mon–Thurs & Sat
noon–2.30pm & 7–10.30pm, Fri
noon–2.30pm. One of the best
vegetarian choices in the city,
with a moderately priced and
inventive menu full of high-
class, organic, vegetarian choices.

Le Reminet

3 rue des Grands Degrés
☎01.44.07.04.24. Mon & Thurs–Sun
noon–2.30pm &7.30–11pm; closed
two weeks in Aug. Snowy-white
tablecloths and fancy chandeliers
add a touch of class to this little
bistro-restaurant, and imaginative sauces grace high-quality
traditional French ingredients.
By no means a budget bistro,
but excellent value all the same.

Tashi Delek

4 rue des Fossés-St-Jacques
☎01.43.26.55.55. Mon–Sat
noon–2.30pm & 7–11pm; closed two
weeks in Aug. Elegantly styled
Tibetan restaurant serving hearty,
warming noodle soups and the
addictive, ravioli-like *momok*.
There is even yak-butter tea, a
salty, soupy concoction that's an
acquired taste. You can eat well
for remarkably little money.

Bars

Le Piano Vache

8 rue Laplace. Mon–Fri noon–2am, Sat
& Sun 9pm–2am. Venerable bar
crammed with students drinking
at little tables, with French rock
or dance-based music on the
CD-player and a laid-back,
grungey atmosphere.

Les Pipos

2 rue de l'Ecole-Polytechnique.
Mon–Sat 8am–1am; closed two weeks
in Aug. Old, carved wooden bar
in a long-established position
opposite the gates of the former
grande école. Serves well-priced
wines along with simple plates
of Auvergnat charcuterie, cheese
and the like.

Le Violon Dingue

46 rue de la Montagne Ste-Geneviève.
daily 6pm–2.30am, happy hour
8–10pm. A long, dark student
pub that's also popular with
young travellers. Noisy and
friendly, with English-speaking
bar staff and cheap drinks. The
cellar bar stays open until
4.30am on busy nights.

Live music

Caveau de la Huchette

5 rue de la Huchette ☎01.43.26.65.05.
A wonderful slice of old
Parisian life in an otherwise
touristy area. Live jazz, usually
trad and big band, to dance to
on a floor surrounded by tiers
of benches. Daily 9.30pm–2am,
but best at weekends. Entrance
around €15.

St-Germain

St-Germain, the westernmost section of Paris's Left Bank, has long been famous as the haunt of bohemians and intellectuals. A few well-known cafés preserve a strong flavour of the old times, but the dominant spirit these days is elegant, relaxed and seriously upmarket. At opposite ends of the quarter are two of the city's busiest and best-loved sights: to the east, bordering the Quartier Latin, spread the exquisite lawns of the **Jardin du Luxembourg**, while to the west stands the **Musée d'Orsay**, a converted railway station with a world-beating collection of Impressionist paintings. Between the two, you can visit the churches of **St-Sulpice** and **St-Germain-des-Prés**, or intriguing museums dedicated to the artists **Delacroix** and **Maillol**, but really, **shopping** is king. The streets around place St-Sulpice swarm with international fashion brands, while on the north side of boulevard St-Germain antique shops and art dealers dominate. Between shopping sprees, you can explore the *quartier*'s excellent **cafés and bars**, among which you'll find some Parisian classics.

Pont des Arts

The delicate and much-loved Pont des Arts was installed in Napoleon's time. It offers a classic upstream view of the Ile de la Cité, and also provides a grand entrance to St-Germain under the watchful eye of the Institut de France, an august academic institution whose members are known as "Immortals".

The Jardin du Luxembourg

Daily dawn to dusk. Fronting onto rue de Vaugirard, Paris's longest street, the Jardin du Luxembourg is the chief lung of the Left Bank. Its atmosphere is a beguiling mixture of formal and utterly relaxed. At the park's centre, the perfectly round pond and immaculate floral parterres are overlooked by the haughty **Palais du Luxembourg**, the seat of the French Senate. Elsewhere,

students sprawl about on the garden's famous metal chairs, children sail toy yachts, watch the puppets at the *guignol*, or run about in the playgrounds, and old men gather to play boules or chess. In summer, the most contested spots are the shady **Fontaine de Médicis** in the northeast corner, and the lawns of the southernmost strip – one of the few areas where you're allowed to lie out on the grass. The quieter, wooded southwest corner is dotted with the works

▼ JARDIN DU LUXEMBOURG

▼ ST-GERMAIN STREET SCENE

Deux Magots is all that remains of a once-enormous Benedictine monastery. Inside the adjoining church of St-Germain-des-Prés, the transformation from Romanesque nave to early Gothic choir is just about visible under the heavy green and gold nineteenth-century paintwork. The last chapel on the south side contains the tomb of the philosopher René Descartes, while in the corner of the churchyard by rue Bonaparte, a little Picasso sculpture of a woman's head is dedicated to the poet Apollinaire.

of famous sculptors, and ends in a miniature orchard of elaborately espaliered pear trees.

Musée du Luxembourg

19 rue de Vaugirard ☎01.42.34.25.95, ⓦwww.museeduluxembourg.fr. The Musée du Luxembourg lies at the top end of Paris's longest street, rue de Vaugirard, backing onto the park. It holds temporary art exhibitions that rank among the most ambitious in Paris – recent shows have included Raphael, Gauguin, Modigliani and Botticelli. Check for opening hours.

Place St-Germain-des-Prés

The hub of the *quartier* is place St-Germain-des-Prés, with the famous café *Les Deux Magots* on one corner, and *Café Flore* and *Brasserie Lipp* just a stone's throw away. All three are renowned for the number of intellectual and literary backsides that have shined their seats, and are expensive and extremely crowded in summer.

St-Germain-des-Prés

Place St-Germain-des-Prés. Daily 7.30am–7.30pm. The ancient tower overlooking place St-Germain-des-Prés opposite *Les*

Musée Delacroix

6 rue de Furstenberg ⓦwww.musee-delacroix.fr. Daily except Tues 9.30am–5pm. €4. The Musée Delacroix occupies the house where the artist lived and worked from 1857 until his death in 1863, and still displays his paintbox alongside other curiosities and personal effects. Although Delacroix's major work is exhibited permanently at the Louvre (see p.76) and the Musée d'Orsay (see p.132), this museum displays a refreshingly intimate collection of small-scale paintings, watercolours, drawings and frescoes, and holds good temporary exhibitions on Delacroix and his contemporaries.

St-Sulpice

Place St-Sulpice. Daily 7.30am–7.30pm. It took over a hundred years to build the enormous church of St-Sulpice, and it remains incomplete, with uncut masonry blocks still protruding from the south tower, awaiting the sculptor's chisel. The facade is rather overpoweringly classical, but any severity is softened by the chestnut trees and fountain of the peaceful

place St-Sulpice, and the crowds
at the outside tables of the *Café
de la Mairie*, on the sunny side of
the square. The best thing about
the gloomy interior are the
three Delacroix murals,
including one of St Michael

slaying a dragon, found in the
first chapel on the right.

The rue Mabillon grid

The miniature group of streets
immediately north of St-Sulpice
– rue des Canettes, rue

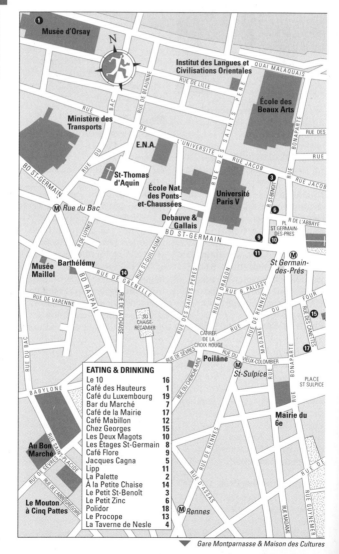

EATING & DRINKING

Le 10	16
Café des Hauteurs	1
Café du Luxembourg	19
Bar du Marché	7
Café de la Mairie	17
Café Mabillon	12
Chez Georges	15
Les Deux Magots	10
Les Étages St-Germain	8
Café Flore	9
Jacques Cagna	5
Lipp	11
La Palette	2
À la Petite Chaise	14
Le Petit St-Benoît	3
Le Petit Zinc	6
Polidor	18
Le Procope	13
La Taverne de Nesle	4

Princesse and rue Mabillon – is particularly glossy, with lots of rather expensive bistrot restaurants, little boutiques and bars packed into the pretty old houses. The main attraction, however, is the array of fashion boutiques, which start with Agnès B and the very elegant Yves Saint Laurent Rive Gauche on the corner of place St-Sulpice itself, and spread west from there.

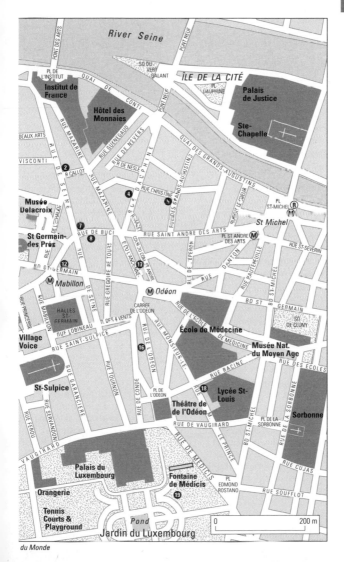

Musée Maillol

61 rue de Grenelle ⓦ www
.museemailloil.com. Daily except Tues
11am–6pm. €7. An outwardly
inconspicuous eighteenth-
century house is now the home
of the Musée Maillol, its
interior bursting with Aristide
Maillol's buxom sculptures of
female nudes, of which the
smoothly curvaceous
Mediterranean is his most famous.
Other rooms house drawings by
Matisse, Dufy and Bonnard,
humorously erotic paintings by
Bombois, and the odd Picasso,
Degas, Gauguin and Kandinsky.
The museum also organizes
excellent exhibitions of
twentieth-century art, among
which have been Frida Kahlo
and Diego Rivera.

The Musée d'Orsay

1 rue de la Légion d'Honneur
ⓦwww.musee-orsay.fr. Tues–Sun
9am–6pm, Thurs to 9.45pm; mid-Sept
to mid-June opens at 10am. €7
Mon–Sat, €5 Sun, free to under-18s
and on first Sun of the month. Down
on the riverfront, just west of
St-Germain, the Musée d'Orsay
dramatically fills a former
railway station with paintings
and sculptures dating from
between 1848 and 1914,
including an unparalleled
Impressionist and Post-
Impressionist collection. The
museum's **ground floor**, spread
out under the giant glass arch, is
devoted to pre-1870 work,
contrasting Ingres, Delacroix
and other serious-minded
painters with the relatively
wacky works of Puvis de
Chavannes, Gustave Moreau and
the younger Degas. On the
other side of the tracks, as it
were, the Barbizon school and
the Realists prepare the ground
for Impressionism, along with
Monet's violently light-filled

▲ MUSEE D'ORSAY

Femmes au Jardin (1867) and
Manet's provocative *Olympia*
(1863), which heralded the
arrival of the new school.

Impressionism proper packs
the attic-like **upper level**, with
famous images such as Monet's
Poppies and *Femme à l'Ombrelle*,
Manet's *Déjeuner sur l'Herbe*,
Degas' *L'Absinthe*, and Renoir's
Bal du Moulin de la Galette.
You'll also find some of Degas'
wonderful sculptures of ballet-
dancers and a host of
small-scale landscapes and
outdoor scenes by Renoir,
Sisley, Pissarro and Monet that
owed much of their brilliance
to the novel practice of setting
up easels in the open. More
heavyweight masterpieces can
be found by Monet and Renoir
in their middle and late periods,
Van Gogh and Cézanne, as well
as a dimly lit section devoted to
pastels by Degas, Redon,
Manet, Mondrian and others.
The final suite of rooms on this
level begins with Rousseau's
dreamlike *La Charmeuse de
Serpent* (1907) and continues
past Gauguin's ambivalent
Tahitian paintings to Pointillist
works by Seurat, Signac and
others, ending with Toulouse-

Lautrec at his caricaturial nightclubbing best.

Down on the **middle level** is a disparate group of paintings, including the Art Nouveau Nabis, notably Bonnard and Vuillard, some international Symbolist paintings, and lots of late-nineteenth-century painting from the naturalist schools.

Bridging the parallel sculpture terraces, the **Rodin terrace** puts almost everything else to shame. Finally, try to spare some energy for the half-dozen adjacent rooms filled with superb Art Nouveau furniture and *objets d'art*.

Shops

Au Bon Marché

38 rue de Sèvres. Mon–Fri 9.30am–7pm, Sat to 8pm. The oldest department store in Paris, founded in 1852, and one of its most upmarket – in fact, it's famous for having a name meaning the opposite of what it really is (*bon marché* in French means "cheap"). The food hall is legendary and there's an excellent kids' department.

Barthélemy

51 rue de Grenelle. Tues–Sat 8am–1pm & 4–7.15pm; closed Aug. Purveyors of cheeses to the rich and powerful. Madame Bathélemy herself is on hand in the mornings to offer expert advice on choosing and caring for your cheese.

Debauve & Gallais

30 rue des Sts-Pères
ⓦwww.debauve-et -gallais.com. Mon–Sat 9am–7pm; closed Aug. This beautiful, ancient shop specializes in exquisite, expensive dark chocolates. Open since 1800, it now offers an e-shopping service.

Le Mouton à Cinq Pattes

Men 138 bd St-Germain, women 8 & 18 rue St-Placide. Mon–Sat 10am–7pm. A classic bargain clothing address, with racks upon racks of end-of-line and reject clothing from designer names both great and small. You might find a shop-soiled Gaultier classic; you might find nothing. At these prices, it's worth the gamble.

Poilâne

8 rue du Cherche-Midi. Mon–Sat 7.15am–8.15pm. This extremely classy bakery is the ultimate source of the famous "Pain Poilâne", and a great place for other bakery treats, too.

Village Voice

6 rue Princesse. Mon 2–8pm, Tues–Sat 10am–8pm, Sun 2–7pm. A welcoming re-creation of an American neighbourhood bookstore, with a good selection of contemporary fiction and non-fiction, and a decent list of British and American poetry and classics.

▼ POILANE BAKERY

Cafés

Bar du Marché

75 rue de Seine. Daily 7am–2am.
Humming café where the waiters
are funkily kitted out in flat caps
and bright aprons. Admittedly, you
pay a little extra for the location
near the rue de Buci market.

Café des Hauteurs

Musée d'Orsay, Upper Level. Mon–Wed
& Fri–Sun 10am–5pm, Thurs
10am–9pm. This café in the
Musée d'Orsay has a summer
terrace and a wonderful view of
Montmartre through the giant
railway clock. Serves tea, cakes,
sandwiches and snacks.

Café du Luxembourg

Hours vary according to park opening
times. This delightful, tree-
shaded *buvette* serves hot and
cold drinks right through the
day. Situated northeast of the
pond, in the heart of the Jardin
du Luxembourg. Prices are
high, but not unfairly so.

Café de la Mairie

Place St-Sulpice. Mon–Sat 7am–2am.
Situated on the north side of
the square, this not unduly
pricey café is famous for the
beautiful people sun-seeking on
the outdoor *terrasse*.

Les Deux Magots

170 bd St-Germain. Daily 7.30am–1am.
Right on the corner of place St-
Germain-des-Prés, this expensive
café is the victim of its own
reputation as the historic hang-
out of Left Bank intellectuals, but
it's still great for people-watching.

Café Flore

172 bd St-Germain. Daily 7am–1.30am.
The great rival and immediate
neighbour of *Les Deux Magots*.
Sartre, de Beauvoir and Camus
used to hang out here, and it

▲ LES DEUX MAGOTS

keeps up a fashionable, vaguely
intellectual reputation. Best
enjoyed in the late-afternoon
sunshine, or upstairs among the
regulars. Beware of the prices.

Le Procope

13 rue de l'Ancienne-Comédie. Daily
noon–1am. Opened in 1686 as
the first establishment to serve
coffee in Paris, it is still a great
place to enjoy a cup and bask in
the knowledge that over the
years Voltaire, Benjamin
Franklin, Rousseau, Marat and
Robespierre, among others, have
done the very same thing.
Decent but rather overpriced
meals are served, too.

Bars

Le 10

10 rue de l'Odéon. Daily 6pm–2am.
Classic Art Deco-era posters line
the walls of this small dark bar,
and the theme is continued in
the atmospheric cellar bar,
where there's a lot of chatting-
up among the studenty and
international clientele.

Café Mabillon

164 bd St-Germain. Daily
7.30am–6.30am. Posey café-bar that
pulls in modish Parisians and

international types. Best for a quick, pricey cocktail.

Chez Georges

11 rue des Canettes. Tues–Sat noon–2am; closed Aug. Deeply old-fashioned, tobacco-stained wine bar with its old shopfront still in place. The downstairs bar attracts a younger, beery crowd that stays lively well into the small hours. Relatively inexpensive for the area.

Les Etages St-Germain

5 rue de Buci. Daily 11am–2am. Outpost of boho trendiness at the edge of the rue de Buci street market, with a certain trashy glamour. The downstairs café-bar is open to the street, and in the evenings you can lounge around upstairs with a cocktail.

La Taverne de Nesle

32 rue Dauphine. Mon–Thurs & Sun 6pm–4am, Fri & Sat to 5am. Full of local night owls fuelled up by happy hour cocktails (at around €7) and beers (just over €3). Gets busier during student terms, especially at weekends when DJs take to the decks.

Restaurants

Jacques Cagna

14 rue des Grands-Augustins ☎01.43.26.49.39, ⦿www.jacques cagna.com. Mon & Sat 7–10.30pm, Tues–Fri noon–2pm & 7–10.30pm Classy surroundings for very classy and very expensive food – beef with Périgord truffles and the like. The midday menu, however, is relatively inexpensive for cuisine at this level.

Lipp

151 bd St-Germain. Daily noon–1am. One of the most celebrated of all the classic Paris brasseries, and still

the haunt of the successful and famous, with a wonderful 1900s wood-and-glass interior. *Plats du jour*, including the famous sauerkraut, are decent and not overpriced, but the full menu is very expensive. No reservations, so be prepared to wait.

A la Petite Chaise

36 rue de Grenelle ☎01.42.22.13.35. Daily noon–2.30pm & 7.30–10.30pm. Refined, upmarket bistro with an elegant decor. The simple, good-value menu gives centre stage to the food: classic, carefully cooked French dishes, with lots of duck and foie gras.

Le Petit St-Benoît

4 rue St-Benoît ☎01.42.60.27.92. Mon–Sat noon–2.30pm & 7–10.30pm. A tobacco-stained St-Germain institution where aproned servers deliver hearty and, at times, quite heavy traditional fare. Reasonable value for the location.

Polidor

41 rue Monsieur le Prince ☎01.43.26.95.34. Mon–Sat noon–2.30pm & 7pm–12.30am, Sun noon–2.30pm & 7–11pm. A traditional bistro, open since 1845, whose visitors' book, they say, boasts more of history's big names than all the glittering palaces put together. Packed with noisy regulars until late in the evening enjoying meaty Parisian classics on the excellent-value menus. Lunch is a real bargain.

Live music

Maison des Cultures du Monde

101 bd Raspail ☎01.45.44.72.30, ⦿www .mcm.asso.fr. Showcases all the arts from all over the world. Also runs its own world music label, Inedit, and holds a festival of world theatre and music in March.

The Eiffel Tower area

Between St-Germain and the Eiffel Tower, the atmosphere of the Left Bank changes. Gone are the little boutique bars and bistro-restaurants, and in their place are elegant aristocratic mansions and some of the city's most magnificent public monuments. The Eiffel Tower dominates the entire area, its giant scale matched by the sweeping lawns of the Champs de Mars, the 109-metre arch of the Pont Alexandre III and the great military edifices of Les Invalides and the Ecole Militaire. But it's not all inhuman in scale. Right at the foot of the Tower is the village-like oasis of shops and restaurants around the rue Cler market.

The Eiffel Tower

Daily: mid-June to Aug 9am–midnight; Sept to mid-June 9.30am–11pm. Top level €10.20; second level €7, or €3.30 by stairs; first level €3.70. @www.tour-eiffel.fr. It's hard to believe that the Eiffel Tower, the quintessential symbol both of Paris and the brilliance of industrial engineering, was designed to be a temporary structure for a fair, the 1889 Exposition Universelle. When completed, the tower was the tallest building in the world, at 300m. Outraged critics protested against this "grimy factory chimney", though Eiffel himself (not surprisingly) thought it was beautiful in its sheer structural efficiency: "To a certain extent," he wrote, the tower was formed by the wind itself."

Unless you get there ahead of the opening times, or go on a cloudy or rainy day, you're bound to queue at the bottom, for lifts at the changeovers, and again when descending. It's absolutely worth it, however, not just for the view, but for the sheer exhilaration of being inside the structure. The views are usually clearer from the second level, but there's something irresistible about taking the lift all the way up (though be sure to arrive well before 10.30pm, when access to the lifts is closed; note too that the stairs to the second level close at 6pm from Sept to mid-June). Paris looks surreally microscopic from the top, the boulevards looking like leafy canyons and the parks and cemeteries like oases of green. The paint scheme may now be dull brown, but the lighting is

▼ THE EIFFEL TOWER

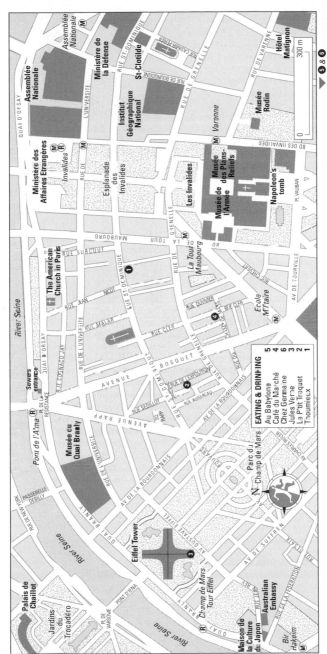

EATING & DRINKING

Au Babylone	5
Café du Marché	4
Chez Germaine	6
Jules Verne	3
La P'tit Troquet	2
Thoumieux	1

more spectacular than ever. The dramatic sweeping searchlight that originally crowned the top has been restored, and for the first ten minutes of every hour from dusk until 2am (1am in winter), thousands of miniature lamps strobe on and off, making the whole structure explode with effervescent light.

The Sewers

May–Sept Mon–Wed, Sat & Sun 11am–5pm; rest of year Mon–Wed, Sat & Sun 11am–4pm. €3.80. On the northeast side of the busy junction of place de la Résistance, is the entrance to one of Paris's more unique attractions a small, visitable section of the sewers, or *les égouts*. Once you're underground it's dark, damp and noisy with gushing water, but children may be disappointed to find that it's not too smelly. The main part of the visit runs along a gantry walk poised above a main sewer, displaying photographs, lamps, specialized sewermen's tools and other antique flotsam and jetsam which turn the history of the city's water supply and waste management into a surprisingly fascinating topic. What the display doesn't tell you is that the work isn't quite finished. Around thirty times a year parts of the system get overloaded with rainwater, and the sewermen have to empty the excess – waste and all – straight into the Seine.

Rue Cler and around

A little further upstream still, the American Church on quai d'Orsay, together with the American College nearby at 31 av Bosquet, is a nodal point in the well-organized life of Paris's large American

▲ LES INVALIDES

community, its noticeboard usualy plastered with job and accommodation offers and demands.

Just to the south, and in stark contrast to the austerity of much of the rest of the quarter, is the attractive, villagey wedge of early nineteenth-century streets between avenue Bosquet and the Invalides. Chief among them is rue Cler, whose food shops act as a kind of permanent market. The cross-streets, rue de Grenelle and rue St-Dominique, are full of neighbourhood shops, posh *bistrots* and little hotels.

Les Invalides

ⓦwww.invalides.org. There's no missing the overpowering facade of the Hôtel des Invalides, topped by its resplendently gilded dome. It was built on the orders of Louis XIV as a home for wounded soldiers, and part of the building is still used as a hospice, along with the soldiers' church. The rest houses Napoleon's tomb, in the Eglise du Dôme, and a suite of museums, the most interesting of which are detailed separately below.

Musée de l'Armée

Daily: April–Sept 10am–6pm, Oct–March 10am–5pm. €7, ticket also valid for Napoleon's tomb. The most fascinating section of this vast national army museum is devoted to World War II. The battles, the resistance and the slow liberation are documented through imaginatively displayed war memorabilia combined with gripping reels of contemporary footage, many of which have an English-language option. One leaves shocked, stirred, and with the distinct impression that Général de Gaulle was personally responsible for the liberation of France. The beautiful collection of medieval and Renaissance armour in the west wing of the royal courtyard is well worth admiring, though note that large areas are shut for renovation until late 2005. Over in the east wing, the wearyingly large collection of later uniforms and weapons, however, is probably for military history buffs only.

Musée des Plans-Reliefs

Same hours and ticket as Musée de l'Armée. Up under the roof of the east wing, the Musée des Plans-Reliefs displays an extraordinary collection of super-scale models of French ports and fortified cities, created in the seventeenth and eighteenth centuries to aid military planning. With the eerie green glow of their landscapes only just illuminating the long, tunnel-like attic, the effect is distinctly chilling.

Napoleon's tomb

Same hours and ticket as Musée de l'Armée. Some visitors find the Eglise du Dôme gloriously sumptuous, others think it's supremely pompous. Either way, it's overwhelming. Sunk into the floor at the centre is Napoleon's tomb, a giant red porphyry sarcophagus, enclosed within a gallery emblazoned with Napoleonic quotations of awesome but largely truthful conceit. When Napoleon was finally interred here, on a

▼ RUE ST-DOMINIQUE

▲ NAPOLEON'S TOMB

freezing cold day in 1840, half a million Parisians came to watch his last journey. Victor Hugo commented: "It felt as if the whole of Paris had been poured to one side of the city, like liquid in a vase which has been tilted."

Musée Rodin

Tues–Sun: April–Sept 9.30am–5.45pm, garden closes 6.45pm; Oct–March 9.30am–4.45pm, garden closes 5pm. €5 or €1 for garden only. The captivating Musée Rodin is housed in the eighteenth-century mansion where the sculptor died in November 1917. Bronze versions of major projects like *The Burghers of Calais*, *The Thinker*, and *The Gate of Hell* are exhibited in the garden, while smaller-scale works are housed indoors, their raw energy offset by the hôtel's elegant wooden panelling, tarnished mirrors and chandeliers. The museum is usually very crowded with visitors eager to see well-loved works such as *The Hand of God* and *The Kiss*, but it's well worth lingering by the vibrant, impressionistic clay and plaster works, small studies done from life at Rodin's own hand – after completing his apprenticeship Rodin rarely picked up a chisel, as in the nineteenth century it was normal for artists to delegate the task of working up stone and bronze versions to assistants. On the ground floor, a room is devoted to Camille Claudel, Rodin's pupil, model and lover – look out for the sculpture *The Age of Maturity*, which symbolises her ultimate rejection by Rodin.

▲ MUSEE RODIN

Restaurants

Au Babylone

13 rue de Babylone ☎01.45.48.72.13.
Mon–Sat noon–2.30pm; closed Aug.
Lots of old-fashioned charm
and culinary basics such as *steak-frites* on the reasonably priced
menu.

Café du Marché

38 rue Cler ☎01.47.05.51.27.
Mon–Sat noon–11pm. Big, busy
café-brasserie in the heart of the
rue Cler market serving
excellent-value meals, with
good, market-fresh *plats du jour*.

Chez Germaine

30 rue Pierre-Leroux
☎01.42.73.28.34. Mon–Fri
noon–2.30pm & 7–9.30pm, Sat
noon–2.30pm; closed Aug. A simple
and tiny restaurant that packs
them in for the excellent value,
inexpensive lunchtime menu.
You can see it's all freshly
cooked because it's all done
right in front of you.

Jules Verne

Eiffel Tower ☎01.45.55.61.44.
12.15–1.45pm & 7.15–9.45pm.
Genuinely haute cuisine – served
in the second-floor restaurant of
the Eiffel Tower in a moodily

designed, modern space with lots
of romantic corners. Book three
months in advance for the
exceptional, highly adventurous
cuisine and, of course, the views.
Lunch menu at €49 (weekdays
only), evening menu at €110.

Le P'tit Troquet

28 rue de l'Exposition
☎01.47.05.80.39. Tues–Sat
12.30–2.30pm & 7.30–10.30pm.
Decked out like an elegant
antiques shop, this tiny family
restaurant is a very discreet
place, serving refined cuisine to
the diplomats and politicians of
the *quartier*. Expect to pay
upwards of €30.

Thoumieux

79 rue St-Dominique
☎01.47.05.49.75. Daily
noon–3.30pm & 6.30pm–midnight.
This cavernous, traditional
brasserie is replete with
mirrors, carved wood, hatstands
and bustling, black-and-white
clad waiters. It's popular with a
smart local clientele for the
carefully prepared classic
dishes, many from the
southwest of France. The basic
lunch menu is inexpensive, but
you'll pay over €30 in the
evening.

Montparnasse

Montparnasse has been Paris's place of play for centuries. The entertainments today are mostly glitzy cinemas and late-opening restaurants, but between the wars the celebrated cafés on the boulevard du Montparnasse were filled with fashionable writers and artists such as Picasso, Matisse, Man Ray, Modigliani, Giacometti and Chagall. The most animated stretch of the boulevard begins at the ugly brown skyscraper, the Tour Montparnasse, and ends at boulevard Raspail, where Rodin's hulking statue of *Balzac* broods over the traffic. You can climb the tower for fantastic views or, for a complete contrast, descend into the grisly catacombs in the old quarries of Denfert-Rochereau. To hunt down Montparnasse's artistic past, visit the excellent, intimate museums dedicated to the sculptors Zadkine and Bourdelle, or the old studios that now house the gallery and exhibition space of the Musée de Montparnasse. Modern art – not to mention modern architecture – has its own cool venue, the superb Fondation Cartier, while the Fondation Cartier-Bresson puts on photography exhibitions.

The Tour Montparnasse

April–Sept daily 9.30am–11.30pm; Oct–March Mon–Thurs & Sun 9.30am–10.30pm, Fri 9.30am–11.30pm. €8 to 59th-floor tower-top, €7 to 56th floor gallery room. ⓦwww.tourmontparnasse56 .com. The two-hundred-metre-tall Tour Montparnasse may be one of the city's least-liked landmarks, but it offers fabulous views from the top – though its most vehement opponents say this is only because the tower you're standing on doesn't spoil the view. Carping aside, the panorama is arguably better than the one from the Eiffel Tower – after all, it has the Eiffel Tower in it, plus it also costs less to ascend and there are no queues. Sunset is the best time for the trip, and you could always treat yourself to a pricey drink in the 56th-storey bar.

Jardin Atlantique

Access by lifts on rue Cdt. R. Mouchotte and bd Vaugirard, or by the stairs alongside platform #1 in Montparnasse station. Montparnasse

▼ TOUR MONTPARNASSE

PLACES

Montparnasse

▲ JARDIN ATLANTIQUE

station was once the great arrival and departure point for travellers across the Atlantic, and for Bretons seeking work in the capital. The connection is commemorated in the extraordinary Jardin Atlantique, a sizeable park that the city planners have actually suspended on top of the train tracks, between cliff-like, high-

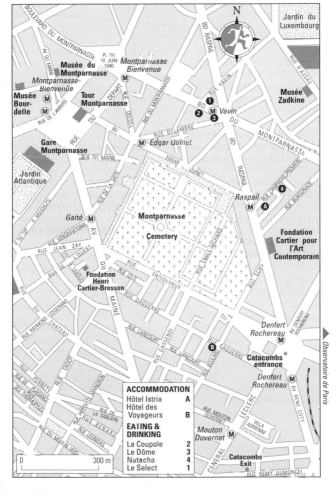

ACCOMMODATION

| Hôtel Istria | A |
| Hôtel des Voyageurs | B |

EATING & DRINKING

La Coupole	2
Le Dôme	3
Natacha	4
Le Select	1

0 _____ 300 m

Observatoire de Paris

rise apartment blocks. The park's design is a classic example of Parisian flair, with a field of Atlantic-coast grasses, wave-like undulations in the lawn, whimsical, electronically controlled fountains and sculptural areas hidden among trees.

Musée du Montparnasse

21 avenue du Maine. Tues–Sun noon–7pm. €5. Picasso, Léger, Modigliani, Chagall, Braque and other members of the Montparnasse group of artists from the first half of the twentieth century used to come to dine at what was once the *Cantine des Artistes*, a canteen and studio run by Marie Vassilieff. The venue now hosts the Musée du Montparnasse, which displays excellent exhibitions of work by Montparnasse artists, past and present. The gallery lies at the end of a secretive, ivy-clad alley, an attractive remnant of the interwar years that is still used for studio space – though mostly by expensive architects nowadays.

Musée Bourdelle

16–18 rue A. Bourdelle. Tues–Sun 10am–6pm. Free. Large-scale, heroic-looking modern sculptures loom over the small, street-front courtyard of the Musée Bourdelle, providing a good taste of what's inside. The museum was created around the former *atelier* of the early twentieth-century sculptor, Antoine Bourdelle, and the highlight of the visit is the artist's atmospheric old **studio**, littered with half-complete works and musty with the smells of its ageing parquet floor. You can also visit Bourdelle's living quarters,

complete with shabby bed, stove and some sombre paintings from his private collection. The rest of the museum is more conventional, a showpiece for Bourdelle's half-naturalistic, half-geometrical style – he was Rodin's pupil and Giacometti's teacher, after all.

Musée Zadkine

100 bis rue d'Assas. Tues–Sun 10am–6pm. €3.30. The cottage-like home and garden studios of Cubist sculptor Ossip Zadkine, where he lived and worked from 1928 to 1967, are now overshadowed by tall buildings on all sides, and occupied by the tiny but satisfying Musée Zadkine. A mixture of slender, elongated figures and blockier, harder-edged works are displayed in just a handful of intimate-sized rooms, while the sculptor's Cubist bronzes are scattered about the minuscule garden, sheltering under trees or emerging from clumps of bamboo. The site is low-key, but invites contemplative lingering.

Fondation Cartier pour l'Art Contemporain

261 bd Raspail. Tues–Sun noon–8pm. €5. The Fondation Cartier pour l'Art Contemporain is a stunningly translucent construction designed by Jean Nouvel in 1994. A bold wall of glass follows the line of the street, attached by thin steel struts to the building proper, which is also built almost entirely of glass. All kinds of contemporary art – installations, videos, multi-media – often by foreign artists little known in France, are shown in temporary exhibitions that use the building's light and very generous spaces to maximum advantage. Photographer Herb

Ritts has had his work showcased here, Issey Miyake has experimented with fabric designs, and a group of artists and photographers has collaborated on an exhibition inspired by the Amazonian Yanomami people.

Montparnasse cemetery

Mid-March to Oct Mon–Fri 8am–6pm, Sat 8.30am–6pm, Sun 9am–6pm; Nov–March closes 5.30pm.

Fascinating rather than gloomy, Montparnasse cemetery is filled with ranks of miniature temples whose architecture ranges from the austere to the utterly sentimental. There are plenty of illustrious names to chase up, too.

To the right of the entrance, by the wall, is the unembellished joint grave of Jean-Paul Sartre and Simone de Beauvoir. Sartre lived out the last few decades of his life just a few metres away on boulevard Raspail. Down avenue de l'Ouest, which follows the western wall of the cemetery, you'll find the tombs of Baudelaire, the painter Soutine, Dadaist Tristan Tzara, Zadkine,

and the Fascist Pierre Laval, a member of Pétain's government who, after the war, was executed for treason, not long after a suicide attempt. As an antidote, you can pay homage to Proudhon, the anarchist who coined the phrase "Property is theft!"; he lies in Division 1, by the Carrefour du Rond-Point.

In the southwest corner of the cemetery is an old windmill, which housed a famously raucous tavern in the seventeenth century.

Across rue Emile-Richard, in the eastern section of the cemetery, lie car-maker André Citroën, Guy de Maupassant, César Franck, and the celebrated victim of French anti-Semitism at the end of the nineteenth century, Captain Dreyfus. Right in the northern corner is a tomb with a sculpture by Brancusi, *The Kiss*. Its depiction of two people, locked in an embrace, sculpted from the same piece of stone, speaks of an undying love, and makes a far more poignant statement than the dramatic and passionate scenes of grief adorning so many of the other graves.

▲ MONTPARNASSE CEMETERY

Fondation Henri Cartier-Bresson

Impasse Lebouis. Wed 1–8.30pm, Thurs, Fri & Sun 1–6.30pm, Sat 11am–6.45pm; closed Aug. €4. Ⓦ www.henricartierbresson.org. Old-fashioned networks of streets still exist in the Pernety and Plaisance *quartiers*, immediately south of Montparnasse cemetery. It's an appropriately atmospheric location for the Fondation Henri Cartier-Bresson, which puts on excellent photography exhibitions, alternating with shows of the work of the great Parisian photojournalist, Henri Cartier-Bresson.

The Catacombs

Place Denfert-Rochereau. Tues–Sun 10am–4pm. €5. Paris's catacombs are frankly weird. The entrance in the middle of busy place Denfert-Rochereau – formerly place d'Enfer, or "Hell Square" – takes you down into what was once an underground quarry, but is now a series of tunnels lined with seemingly endless heaps of human bones. It's estimated that the remains of six million Parisians are interred here, which is more than double the population of the modern city (not counting the suburbs). The bones originally came from Paris's old charnel houses and cemeteries, which had become overstocked health hazards and were cleared between 1785 and 1871. The fact that the long femurs and skulls are stacked in elaborate geometric patterns makes the effect bizarre rather than spooky, and few visitors find the experience genuinely unsettling. Older children often love it, but there are a good couple of kilometres to walk, and it can quickly become claustrophobic, not to mention cold and gungy underfoot.

Cafés

Le Dôme

108 bd du Montparnasse. Daily: restaurant noon–3pm & 7pm–12.30am; café 8am–1.30am. Another haunt of artists and writers – Sartre and Hemingway among them – but this one has moved even more seriously

▲ CATACOMBS

▼ LE DOME

upmarket than its nearby brethren. There's wonderful but expensive seafood at the *bistrot*, but you can soak up the atmosphere in the café version, where cinema pictures decorate each alcove.

Le Select

99 bd du Montparnasse. Mon–Thurs & Sun till 3am, Fri & Sat till 4.30am Perhaps not *quite* as famous as its immediate neighbours – the other Montparnasse cafés frequented by Picasso, Modigliani, Cocteau and the rest – but much less spoilt, slightly less expensive and infinitely more satisfying. Perfect for a coffee or just possibly a Cognac.

Restaurants

La Coupole

102 bd du Montparnasse
☎01.43.20.14.20. Daily 8.30am–1am. The largest and perhaps the most enduring arty-chic Parisian hang-out for dining, dancing and debate. The place buzzes with conversation and clatter from the diners packed in tightly under the high, chandeliered roof. The menus are moderately priced at lunch, becoming more expensive in the evening, though if you can wait until 10.30pm you'll be able to take advantage of their great-value late-night version.

Natacha

17 bis rue Campagne-Première
☎01.43.20.79.27. Mon–Sat 8.30pm–1am. This cool, spacious bistro attracts a celebrity crowd. In the kitchen, they introduce warm Mediterranean flavours to traditional Parisian dishes, and there's even a pasta course – very daring. Unrestrained ordering will cost you, but it's possible to get away with a moderate final bill.

Southern Paris

You might not think of venturing into the relatively amorphous swathe of southern Paris, but there are some beguiling, untouched pockets of the old city to explore, as well as an excellent flea market, the Puces de Vanves. Some of the city's loveliest public parks are found on the southernmost fringes of the city, too: the Parc Montsouris has been imaginatively landscaped while the futuristic Parc André-Citroën has its own giant helium balloon, offering fantastic views. There are few sights as such, though you could make the pilgrimage to La Ruche, home to some of the most avant-garde artists, or the Bibliothèque Nationale de France, the gargantuan, hyper-modern national library. In the evening, Chinatown has obvious culinary attractions, while the Butte-aux-Cailles, one of southern Paris's most characterful quarters, offers lots of excellent, relaxed restaurants and bars.

Parc André-Citroën

Balloon rides daily 9am–5pm; call to check weather conditions on the day

℡01.44.26.20.00. Mon–Fri €10, under-12s €5; Sat & Sun €12, under-12s €6. The riverfront south of

▲ PUCES DE VANVES

André-Citroën. It's not a park for traditionalists. There is a central grassy area, but elsewhere are concrete terraces and walled gardens with abstract themes, hothouses and a large platform sprouting a capricious set of automated fountain jets, luring children and occasionally adults to dodge the sudden spurts of water. Best of all is the tethered balloon, which rises and sinks regularly on calm days, taking small groups up for great views of the city.

Puces de Vanves

Av Marc-Sangnier & av Georges Lafenestre. Sat & Sun 7am–1pm. For original finds, the city's best flea market is the Puces de Vanves. It starts at daybreak on weekends, when endless stalls selling trinkets, knick-knacks and miscellaneous collectables are set up in a long line down avenues

the Eiffel Tower bristles with office blocks and miniature skyscrapers, but at the southwestern extreme of the city limits lies the open, landscaped space of the Parc

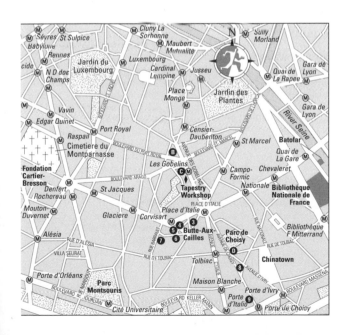

Marc-Sangnier and Georges-Lafenestre. It's well worth the long haul out to the city's southern edge – take Métro line 13 to Porte de Vanves and follow the signs – for an excellent morning's curiosity-shopping.

Allée des Cygnes

Of all the oddball sights in southern Paris, the Allée des Cygnes is probably the most eccentric. It might not sound promising – the "alley" is basically a narrow, embanked concrete avenue lined with trees – but once you've strolled down from the double-decker road and rail bridge, the Pont de Bir-Hakeim, taken in the views of the Eiffel Tower, admired the passing coal barges and visited the small-scale version of the Statue of Liberty at the southern tip of the island, you might just share Samuel Beckett's opinion of the place – it was one of his favourite spots in Paris.

Parc Montsouris

At the southern limits of the city lies the Parc Montsouris. It's a pleasant place to wander, with its winding, contouring paths, its waterfall above the lake and the RER train tracks cutting right through. More surprising features include a meteorological office, a marker of the old meridian line, near boulevard Jourdan, and, by the southwest entrance, a kiosk run by the French Astronomy Association. For a longer walk, you could explore the artistic associations of the immediate neighbourhood. Le Corbusier built the studio at 53 avenue Reille, which runs along the north side of the park, while just off rue Nansouty, the road

▲ BIBLIOTHEQUE NATIONALE DE FRANCE

that follows the park's western edge, lies the secretive and verdant square du Montsouris, and Georges Braque's home on rue Georges Braque. Five minutes' walk to the north, Dalí, Lurçat, Miller and Durrell once lived in the tiny cobbled street of Villa Seurat, off rue de la Tombe-Issoire.

The Butte-aux-Cailles

The almost untouched quartier of the Butte-aux-Cailles, with its little streets and cul-de-sacs of prewar houses and studios, is typical of pre-1960s Paris. The rue de la Butte-aux-Cailles itself is the animated heart of the area, lined with trendy but laid-back bars and restaurants, most of which stay open till the early hours.

Chinatown

You can find Paris's best southeast Asian cuisine in the area that's known as Chinatown, despite the presence of several other east Asian communities. Chinese, Lao, Cambodian, Thai and Vietnamese shops and restaurants fill avenue d'Ivry and avenue de Choisy all the way down to the city limits. The strangest section of the quarter, known as Les Olympiades, is an elevated platform hidden away between giant tower blocks and accessed by escalators from the streets around – rue Nationale, rue de Tolbiac and avenue d'Ivry. At 66 avenue d'Ivry, an escalator climbs up next door to a sliproad leading down to an underground car park; halfway down this access road lurks a tiny Buddhist temple and community centre, advertised by a pair of red Chinese lanterns dimly visible in the gloom.

Bibliothèque Nationale de France

🌐 www.bnf.fr. Tues–Sat 10am–8pm, Sun noon–7pm. €3 for a day pass. The eastern edge of southern Paris, along the riverfront, is in the throes of mammoth development. Chief among the new structures is architect Dominique Perault's Bibliothèque Nationale de France. Four enormous L-shaped towers at the corners of the site mimic open books, and look down on a huge sunken pine wood, with glass walls that filter light into the floors below your feet. There are occasional small-scale exhibitions inside, and the reading rooms on the "haut-jardin" level are open to everyone over 16.

Cafés

L'Entrepôt

7–9 rue Francis-de-Pressensé. Mon–Sat noon–2am. This arts cinema has a spacious, relaxed café with a moody film theme, and outside seating in the courtyard. If you want to eat as well, there are moderately priced, tasty *plats*.

Bars

La Folie en Tête

33 rue de la Butte-aux-Cailles. Mon–Sat 5pm–2am. This is the classic Butte-aux-Cailles address, a laid-back and alternative-spirited bar playing world music and modern French *chanson* and serving beers and coffees to a young, lefty clientele. Cheap drinks and snacks are available in the daytime.

Le Merle Moqueur

11 rue de la Butte-aux-Cailles. Daily 5pm–2am. Tiny bar with a distressed chic ambience, serving up chilled-out music and home-made flavoured rums to young Parisians.

Restaurants

L'Avant Goût

37 rue Bobillot ☎01.45.81.14.06. Tues–Sat noon–2.30pm & 7.30–11pm; closed three weeks in Aug. Small neighbourhood restaurant with a big reputation for exciting modern French cuisine, and wines to match. The contemporary decor, with its red banquettes, and the stylishly presented dishes are distinctly cool. There's a superb-value lunch menu, and you won't pay over the odds in the evening either.

Le Bambou

70 rue Baudricourt ☎01.45.70.91.75. Tues–Sun noon–3pm & 7–10.30pm. Tiny Chinatown bistro crammed with punters tucking into sublimely fresh-tasting, inexpensive Vietnamese food. Serves giant, powerfully flavoured *pho* soups, packed with beef and noodles (choose the large version only if you really mean it), a full menu of

specialities, and their addictive Vietnamese coffee, made with condensed milk.

Le Café du Commerce

51 rue du Commerce
☏01.45.75.03.27. Daily noon–midnight. This deeply old-fashioned brasserie has an unusual setting around a central atrium, with diners served on the balconies at three levels. The menu lists all the classics, with a strong emphasis on meat. Lunch menus are inexpensive, but prices rise somewhat in the evening, though the bill is never excessive.

Chez Gladines

30 rue des Cinq-Diamants
☏01.45.80.70.10. Daily 9am–1am. This tiny corner bistro is always warm and cosy, with a young clientele packed in on rickety tables between the bar and the windows. Serves excellent wines and hearty Basque and southwest dishes such as *magret de canard* or a giant, warm salad with *saucisson* and egg. Filling and excellent value.

▼ CHEZ GLADINES

Le Temps des Cerises

18–20 rue de la Butte-aux-Cailles
☏01.45.89.69.48. Mon–Fri noon–2pm & 7.30–11.45pm, Sat 7.30pm–midnight. Truly welcoming restaurant – it's run as a workers' co-op – with elbow-to-elbow seating and a different daily choice of imaginative dishes. Inexpensive lunch and evening menus, though there are opportunities to splash out a little too.

Tricotin

15 av de Choisy ☏01.45.85.51.52 & ☏01.45.84.74.44. Daily 9.15am–11pm. Glazed in like a pair of overgrown fish tanks, the twin Tricotin restaurants are just set back from the broad avenue de Choisy, at the south end of Chinatown (next to the Chinese-signed McDonald's). Both cover much the same ground, and cover it well and inexpensively. Restaurant no. 1 (closed Tues) specializes in Thai and grilled dishes, while no. 2 has a longer list of Vietnamese, Cambodian and steamed foods.

Clubs

Batofar

Quai de la Gare. Daily 9pm–3am. This old lighthouse boat moored at the foot of the Bibliothèque Nationale is your best bet for a not-too-expensive night out, with a kooky, slightly grungy atmosphere, an eclectic music policy and a diverse clientele. If you don't like the music you hear from the quay, you can also check *Péniche Makara*, or La *Guinguette Pirate*, adjacent. Admission under €10.

Montmartre and northern Paris

One of the most romantic quarters in Paris, **Montmartre** is principally famous for being the home, place of work and playpen of artists such as Renoir, Degas, Picasso and Toulouse-Lautrec. For most of its history, Montmartre was a hilltop village outside the city walls, and today the steep streets around the **Butte Montmartre**, Paris's highest point, preserve an attractively village-like atmosphere. The Butte is topped by the church of **Sacré-Cœur** whose bulbous white domes are visible all over the city. As Montmartre becomes ever more gentrified, brassy **Pigalle** still laps up against the foot of the Butte, its boulevards buzzing with nightspots, ethnic fast-food outlets, cabarets, clubs and, of course, brothels. South again, and in complete contrast, is the genteel and handsome **9e arrondissement**, with its two elegant museums: the **Musée de la Vie Romantique** and the **Musée Moreau**. On the northern edge of the city limits, the mammoth **St-Ouen market** hawks everything from extravagant antiques to the cheapest flea-market hand-me-downs.

The Butte Montmartre

The name "Montmartre" is probably a corruption of Mons Martyrum – the Martyrs' Hill – but its origins may lie farther back with Mons Martis, a Roman shrine to Mars. You can get a dim sense of this pagan past if you stand on top of the Butte Montmartre, the highest point in Paris at 130m, and look down on the sun falling across the valley of the Seine. The quickest way up is by the **funicular**, which is part of the city's Métro system, so passes or Métro tickets can be used. You can also go straight up the steps from square Willette, directly below Sacré-Cœur, but it's more fun to make up a route through the winding streets of Montmartre, a few steps to the west.

▲ ABBESSES METRO

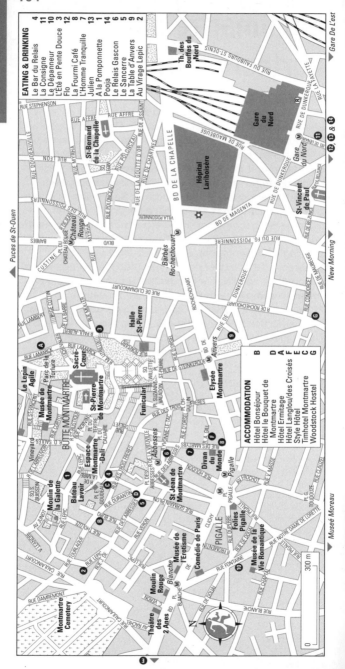

EATING & DRINKING

Le Bar du Relais	4
La Consigne	11
Le Dépanneur	10
L'Été en Pente Douce	3
Flo	12
La Fourmi Café	7
L'Homme Tranquille	8
Julien	13
A la Pomponnette	1
Pooja	14
Le Relais Gascon	6
Le Sancerre	5
La Table d'Anvers	9
Au Virage Lepic	2

ACCOMMODATION

Hôtel Bonséjour	B
Hôtel le Bouquet de Montmartre	D
Hôtel Ermitage	A
Hôtel Langlou/des Croisés	F
Style Hôtel	E
Timhotel Montmartre	C
Woodstock Hostel	G

Place des Abbesses

Postcard-pretty place des Abbesses has one of the only two original Guimard Art-Nouveau Métro entrances that survive intact. The streets immediately around the square are relatively chi-chi for Montmartre, with lots of boutique clothing shops – this is a good area for fashion exploration if you're after one-off outfits and accessories. From here you can head up rue de la Vieuville, from where the stairs in rue Drevet lead to the minuscule place du Calvaire, which has a lovely view back over the city.

Moulin de la Galette

On rue Lepic stands the imposing, wooden Moulin de la Galette. This is one of only two survivors of Montmartre's forty-odd windmills, and once held fashionable dances – as immortalized by Renoir in his *Bal du Moulin de la Galette*, which hangs in the Musée d'Orsay

Place Emile-Goudeau

Halfway up steep, curving rue Ravignan is tiny place Emile-Goudeau, where Picasso, Braque and Juan Gris initiated the Cubist movement in an old piano factory known as the Bateau-Lavoir. The current building is actually a faithful reconstruction, but it's still occupied by studios. With its bench and little iron fountain, the *place* is a lovely spot to draw breath on your way up the Butte.

Place du Tertre and St-Pierre-de-Montmartre

The bogus heart of Montmartre, the place du Tertre, is photogenic but

▲ MOULIN DE LA GALETTE

jammed with sightseers, overpriced restaurants and artists selling lurid oils of Paris landmarks. At the east end of the *place*, however, stands the serene church of St-Pierre-de-Montmartre, the oldest in Paris, along with St-Germain-des-Prés. Although much altered since it was built as a Benedictine convent, in the twelfth century, the church still retains its Romanesque and early Gothic character. The four ancient columns inside – two by the door and two in the choir – are probably leftovers from the Roman shrine that stood on the hill, and their capitals date from Merovingian times, as does the cemetery outside.

Sacré-Cœur

Daily 6am–10.30pm. Dome daily 9am–6.30pm. €5 for the dome.
rowning the Butte, Sacré-Cœur is a weird pastiche of Byzantine-style architecture whose white tower and ice-cream-scoop dome has nevertheless become a much-loved part of the Paris skyline. Construction was started in the 1870s on the initiative of the Catholic

▲ VIEW FROM THE SACRE-CŒUR

Church to atone for the "crimes" of the revolutionary Commune, which first attempted to seize power by dominating the heights of Montmartre. There's little to see in the bare, over-sized interior, but climbing up the **dome** gets you almost as high as the Eiffel Tower. The view from the top is fantastic, but best enjoyed early in the morning or later in the afternoon if you don't want to look straight into the sun.

▼ MONTMARTRE STEPS

Musée de Montmartre

12 rue Cortot. Tues–Sun 10am–6pm. €4.50. This pretty, old Montmartre house, occupied at various times by Renoir, Dufy, Suzanne Valadon and her son Utrillo, is now the low-key Musée de Montmartre, where posters, paintings and mock-ups of various period rooms attempt to recall the atmosphere of Montmartre's pioneering heyday. There's a magnificent view from the back over the hilly northern reaches of the city and the tiny Montmartre vineyard, and the shop usually has a few bottles of Montmartre wine, which they sell for around €40.

The Montmartre vineyard area

The streets falling away to the north of the Butte are among the quietest and least touristy in Montmartre, and a good bet for a romantic stroll. Head down past the Montmartre vineyard, which produces some 1500 bottles a year, and the St-Vincent cemetery. From rue du Mont Cenis, just east of the museum, there's a particularly picturesque view north of some typical Montmartre steps, complete with their double handrail running down the centre, and lampposts between.

Montmartre cemetery

Entrance on av Rachel, underneath rue Caulaincourt. March 16–Nov 5 Mon–Fri 8am–6pm, Sat from 8.30am, Sun from 9am; Nov 6 to March 15 closes 5.30pm. Tucked down below street level in the hollow of an old quarry is Montmartre cemetery, a tangle of trees and funerary pomposity that feels more intimate and less melancholy than Père-Lachaise or Montparnasse. The illustrious dead at rest here include Stendhal, Berlioz, Degas, Nijinsky and François Truffaut, as well La Goulue, the dancer at the Moulin Rouge immortalized by Toulouse-Lautrec. Zola's grave, with its recumbent figure of a corpse, is another fascinating one to look out for, though his remains have been transferred to the Panthéon. There's also a large Jewish section by the east wall. By the entrance, look out for a curious, antique cast-iron poorbox (*Tronc pour les Pauvres*).

Puces de St-Ouen

Mon, Sat & Sun 9am–6.30pm weather dependent; many stands closed Mon. The Puces de St-Ouen, spreads beyond the *périphérique* ring road, at the northern edge of the city, between the Porte de St-Ouen and the Porte de Clignancourt. The bulk of the official markets are closer to the latter Métro stop, while the real junk is mostly found towards the former. It's often called the largest flea market in the world, though it's predominantly a proper antiques market, selling mainly furniture but also such fashionable junk as old café counters, telephones, traffic

▲ ST-OUEN FLEA MARKET MURAL

lights, posters, juke boxes and petrol pumps. Although it's great fun wandering around this section, don't expect any bargains. Each of the twelve official markets within the complex has a slightly different character. Marché Biron is the poshest – Marché Cambo, Marché Antica and Marché Malassis all sell serious and expensive antique furniture. Marché Vernaison – the oldest – has the most diverse collection of old and new furniture and knick-knacks, while Marché Serpette and Marché des Rosiers concentrate on twentieth-century decorative pieces. The relatively new and swish Marché Dauphine has mostly expensive furniture and furnishings, while Marché Paul-Bert, offers all kinds of furniture, china, and the like. Marché Malik stocks mostly discount and vintage clothes, as well as some high-class couturier stuff. Finally, there are Marché Jules-Vallès and Marché Lécuyer-Vallès, which are the cheapest, most junk-like – and most likely to throw up an unexpected treasure.

If you get hungry, make for the classic *restaurant-buvette* in the centre of Marché Vernaison, *Chez Louisette*, where the great gypsy jazz guitarist, Django Reinhardt, sometimes played. The livelier, more rough-and-ready market area is strung out along rue J.H. Fabre and rue du Dr Babinski, under the flyover of the *périphérique* and beyond the boundaries of the market proper. This area is alive with vendors selling cheap clothing and pirated DVDs and endless leather jackets.

Pigalle

The southern slopes of Montmartre are bordered by the broad, busy boulevards de Clichy and de Rochechouart.

The area where the two roads meet, around place Pigalle, has long been a byword for sleaze, with sex shows, sex shops and prostitutes vying for custom. In recent years, however, a resurgence of trendy bars, clubs and music venues have helped rescue Pigalle's reputation.

The Moulin Rouge

82 bd de Clichy ☎01.53.09.82.82, ⓦwww.moulinrouge.fr. The Moulin Rouge is probably the most famous of Paris's cabaret theatres. In the days when Toulouse-Lautrec immortalized

▼ FOLIES PIGALLE

it in his cabaret paintings, it was one of a number of bawdy, populist places of entertainment – as depicted in the blockbuster film. Nowadays, an evening at the cabaret consists of an extremely expensive dinner-and-show formula that attracts coachloads of package-tourists to see the glitz, the special effects and the original feathery can-cans, though there's nothing left of the original atmosphere.

Musée de l'Erotisme

72 bd de Clichy. Daily 10am–2am. €7. Appropriately placed amongst all the sex shops and shows of Pigalle, the Musée de l'Erotisme is testament to its owner's fascination with sex as expressed in folk art. The place is awash with model phalluses, fertility symbols and intertwined figurines from all over Asia, Africa and pre-Columbian Latin America, as well as lots of naughty pictures and statuettes from around Europe. Visiting the museum is by turns an instructive, seedy or hilarious experience, but it's rarely particularly erotic.

Musée de la Vie Romantique

16 rue Chaptal. Tues–Sun 10am–6pm, closed public hols. €6 during exhibitions, otherwise free. The Musée de la Vie Romantique sets out to evoke the era when this quarter was the home of Chopin, Delacroix, Dumas and other prominent figures in the Romantic movement. The house itself, set off a surprising cobbled courtyard, once belonged to the painter Ary Scheffer. George Sand used to visit here, and the ground floor consists mainly of bits and pieces associated with her, including jewels, locks of hair and a cast of her lover Chopin's

surprisingly small hand. Upstairs are a number of Scheffer's sentimental aristocratic portraits.

Musée Moreau

14 rue de La Rochefoucauld. Daily except Tues 10am–12.30pm & 2–5pm. €4. The bizarre and little-visited museum dedicated to the fantastical, Symbolist works of Gustave Moreau was conceived by the artist himself, to be carved out of the house he shared with his parents for many years – you can visit their tiny, stuffy apartments, crammed with furniture and trinkets.
Connected by a beautiful spiral staircase, the two huge, studio-like spaces are no less cluttered: Moreau's canvases hang cheek-by-jowl, every surface crawling with figures and decorative swirls – literally crawling in the case of *The Daughters of Thespius* – or alive with deep colours and provocative symbolism, as in the museum's *pièce de résistance*, *Jupiter and Sémélé*.

Cafés

L'Eté en Pente Douce

23 rue Muller, cnr rue Paul-Albert. Daily noon–midnight. Pure Montmartre atmosphere, with chairs and tables set out beside the long flight of steps that leads up to Sacré-Cœur from the eastern side. Serves decent, fairly inexpensive traditional French *plats*.

Le Sancerre

35 rue des Abbesses. Daily 7am–2am. A fashionable hang-out under the southern slope of Montmartre, with a row of outside tables that's perfect for watching the world go by. The food can be disappointing, so go for a drink, or just the atmosphere on sunny days.

▲ MUSEE MOREAU

Bars

Le Bar du Relais

12 rue Ravignan. Daily 5pm–2am. The decor is quaint and romantic, as is the location just under the Butte, with tables out on the little square. On weekday evenings it's perfect for a glass of wine, while later on, especially at weekends, the music gets cooler and more dance-oriented, and crowds gather outside for cocktails, designer beers and chatter.

Le Dépanneur

27 rue Fontaine. Daily 11am–7am. A relaxed all-night bar, in wood and chrome, just off place Pigalle. One to know about for winding down after clubbing.

La Fourmi Café

74 rue des Martyrs. Mon–Thurs 8am–2am, Fri & Sat 8am–4am, Sun 10am–2am. Trendy but relaxed, this high-ceilinged café-bar has a warm, distressed-bistro decor. It's full of conscientiously beautiful young Parisians drinking coffee by day and beers and cocktails at night.

Montmartre and northern Paris PLACES

Restaurants

L'Homme Tranquille

81 rue des Martyrs ☎01.42.54.56.28.
Mon–Sat 7.30–11.30pm; closed Aug.
Simple and pleasant *bistrot*
ambience, with posters and
nicotine-coloured paint.
Imaginative French dishes on
the moderately priced menu
include chicken in honey,
coriander and lemon.

A la Pomponnette

42 rue Lepic ☎01.46.06.08.36.
Tues–Thurs noon–2.30pm & 7–11pm,
Fri & Sat noon–2.30pm &
7pm–midnight. A genuine old
Montmartre *bistrot*, with posters,
drawings, zinc-top bar, nicotine
stains, etc. The traditional
French food is reliably good, but
expect to pay a little extra for
the location and adorable
atmosphere.

Le Relais Gascon

6 rue des Abbesses ☎01.42.58.58.22.
Daily 10am–2am. A good,
welcoming lunch-stop for
hearty, inexpensive Gascon *plats*
and enormous hot salads.

La Table d'Anvers

2 place d'Anvers ☎01.48.78.35.21.
Noon–2pm & 7–11pm; closed Mon &
Sat lunchtime and Sun. One of the
city's best restaurants, despite the
ugly business-beige decor. A
come-hither menu allows you
to taste the chef's skills without
breaking the bank, but true
gastronomic wining and dining
will set you back a bit.

Au Virage Lepic

61 rue Lepic ☎01.42.52.46.79. Daily
except Tues 7pm–2am. Simple,
good-quality meaty fare served
in a noisy, friendly, old-
fashioned *bistrot*. Small, smoky,
inexpensive and very enjoyable.

La Consigne

2 bd de Denain ☎01.48.78.22.94. Daily
6am–1am, food served to 11pm. A
bog-standard Parisian brasserie,
but usefully located right opposite
the Gare du Nord, and not
overpriced. The waiters are
understandably jaded by the
constant flow of out-of-towners,
but the *plats du jour* are reliable
classics such as *moules frites* and
steak, and there's pleasant seating

▼ LA FOURMI CAFÉ

in the window and on the pavement.

Flo

7 cours des Petites-Ecuries (off rue du Faubourg-St Denis) ☎01.47.70.13.59. Daily noon–3pm & 7pm–1am. Dark, extremely handsome old-time brasserie where you eat elbow to elbow at long tables, served by waiters in ankle-length aprons. Fish and seafood are the specialities, but the food generally is excellent, as is the atmosphere. It's not cheap, but good value for the quality, especially if you come at lunchtime, or pick the menu which includes wine.

Julien

16 rue du Faubourg-St Denis ☎01.47.70.12.06. Daily noon–3pm & 7pm–1am. Part of the same enterprise as the *Flo*, with an even more splendid decor, all globe lamps, hatstands, white linen, brass and polished wood. Serves the same good traditional French cuisine as *Flo*, at the same prices, and it's just as crowded.

Pooja

91 passage Brady (off rue du Faubourg-St Denis) ☎01.48.24.00.83. Mon 6–11pm, Tues–Sun noon–3pm & 6–11pm. Located in a glazed *passage* that is Paris's own slice of the Indian subcontinent, *Pooja* is slightly pricier and sometimes slightly more elaborate than its many inexpensive neighbours, so it probably has the edge – unless you feel like exploring.

Clubs

Elysée Montmartre

72 bd de Rochechouart ⊛www.elyseemontmartre.com. A historic Montmartre nightspot that pulls in a young, excitable crowd with its up-tempo club

nights, held under the huge, arching roof. Every other Saturday there's an unforgettably cheesy, school-disco-style party night called *Le Bal*, with live rock/dance acts and DJs playing 1980s French pop tunes. Frequent gigs midweek.

Folies Pigalle

11 place Pigalle. Tues–Sat midnight–dawn, Sun dawn–midnight. Famed for its sleazy past, and only slightly less sleazy present, the *Folies* is a landmark on the club scene for its house nights and gay-trash "*after*" events early on Saturday morning and right through Sunday.

Live music

Le Divan du Monde

75 rue des Martyrs ☎01.44.92.77.66. The regulars at this deeply famous old café once included Toulouse-Lautrec. Now revived, it's a youthful venue with one of the city's most diverse and exciting programmes, ranging from techno to Congolese rumba, with dancing till dawn on weekend nights.

Le Lapin Agile

22 rue des Saules ☎01.46.06.85.87, ⊛www.au-lapin-agile.com. Tues–Sun 9pm–2am. This old Montmartre artists' haunt features cabaret, poetry and *chanson* nights. Sometimes touristy – it's pricey – but often excellent.

New Morning

7–9 rue des Petites-Ecuries ☎01.45.23.51.41, ⊛www.new morning.com. The place to catch big international names in jazz, as well as aspiring world music acts. There are a few seats, but it's usually a crush of people on the low area in front of the stage.

The Bastille

Now one of Paris's nightlife hotspots, the lively **Bastille quarter** used to be a working-class district, but with the construction of the opera house, the shiny, glass-fronted **Opéra Bastille**, it soon became a magnet for artists and young people. You can still catch some of the working-class flavour east and south of the Bastille, especially along **rue du Faubourg St-Antoine**. Nearby is the **Viaduc des Arts**, an imaginatively converted old railway viaduct whose arches house a wonderful variety of craftshops and *ateliers*, while the disused railway running above has been turned into a delightful green walkway, the **Promenade Plantée**, stretching all the way to the **Bois de Vincennes** on the city's outskirts.

Place de la Bastille

The huge and usually traffic-clogged place de la Bastille is where Parisians congregate to celebrate Bastille Day on July 14, though hardly anything survives of the prison – the few remains have been transferred to square Henri-Galli at the end of boulevard Henri-IV. At the centre of the *place* is a column surmounted by a gilded *Spirit of Liberty*, erected to commemorate not the surrender of the prison, but the July Revolution of 1830 that replaced the autocratic Charles X with the "Citizen King" Louis-Philippe.

Opéra Bastille

120 rue de Lyon ☎08.36.69.78.68, ⓦwww.opera-de-paris.fr. The Bicentennial of the French Revolution, in 1989, was marked by the inauguration of a new opera house on place de la Bastille, the Opéra Bastille. Its reception was rather mixed; the architect, Uruguyan Carlos Ott, was concerned that his design should not bring an overbearing monumentalism to the *place*, and while the different depths and layers of the semicircular facade do give a certain sense of the building stepping back, self-effacing it is not. Time, use and familiarity have more or less reconciled it to its surroundings, though, and people happily sit on its steps, wander into its shops and libraries, and camp out all night for the free performance on July 14.

▼ PLACE DE LA BASTILLE COLUMN

Rue de Lappe

One of the liveliest night-time spots in Paris is rue de Lappe, crammed with animated, young bars, full to bursting on the weekends. *Balajo* at no. 9 is one remnant of a very Parisian tradition: the *bals musettes*, or music halls of 1930s *gai Paris*, frequented between the wars by Piaf, Jean Gabin and Rita Hayworth. Hip cafés and bars have also sprung up in the surrounding streets, elbowing their way in among the fashion boutiques and wacky interior

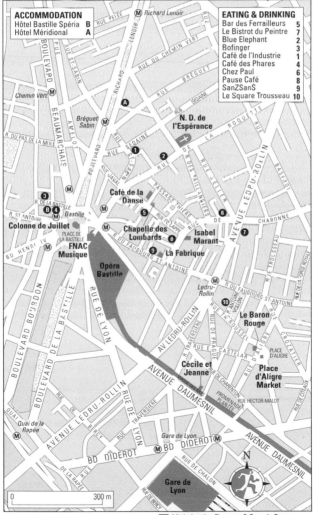

ACCOMMODATION
Hôtel Bastille Spéria B
Hôtel Méridional A

EATING & DRINKING
Bar des Ferrailleurs 5
Le Bistrot du Peintre 7
Blue Elephant 2
Bofinger 3
Café de l'Industrie 1
Café des Phares 4
Chez Paul 6
Pause Café 8
SanZSanS 9
Le Square Trousseau 10

▼ Ministère des Finances & Parc de Bercy

designers on rue de Charonne and the alternative, hippy outfits on rues Keller and de la Roquette.

Rue du Faubourg St-Antoine

The cradle of revolutions and, not coincidentally, principal working-class *quartier* of Paris since the fifteenth century, Rue du Faubourg St-Antoine has traditionally been associated with furniture-making. Many furniture workshops, as well as related trades such as inlayers, stainers and polishers, still inhabit the maze of interconnecting yards and *passages* that run off the faubourg, especially at the western end. One of the most attractive courtyards is at no. 56, with its lemon trees, and ivy- and rose-covered buildings.

Place d'Aligre market

Tues–Sun 7.30am–1pm. The place d'Aligre market, between avenue Daumesnil and rue du Faubourg St-Antoine, is a lively, raucous affair, particularly at weekends. The square itself is given over to clothes and bric-a-brac stalls, selling anything from old gramophone players to odd bits of crockery. It's along the adjoining **rue d'Aligre** where the market really comes to life, though, with the vendors, many of Algerian origin, doing a frenetic trade in fruit and veg.

The Promenade Plantée

The Promenade Plantée, also known as the Coulée Verte, is an excellent way to see a little-visited part of the city – and from an unusual angle. This stretch of disused railway line, much of it along a viaduct, has been ingeniously converted into an elevated walkway and planted with a profusion of trees and flowers – cherry trees, maples, limes, roses and lavender. The walkway starts near the beginning of **avenue Daumesnil**, just south of the Bastille opera house, and is reached via a flight of stone steps – or lifts – with a number of similar access points all the way along. It takes you to the Parc de Reuilly, then descends to ground level and continues nearly as far as the *périphérique*, from where you can follow signs to the Bois de Vincennes. The whole walk is around 4.5km long, but if you don't feel like doing the whole thing you could just walk the first part – along the viaduct – which also happens to be the most attractive stretch, running past venerable old mansion blocks and giving you a bird's eye view of the street below.

▼ PROMENADE PLANTEE

The Viaduc des Arts

The arches of the Promenade Plantée's viaduct itself have had their red brickwork scrubbed clean and have been converted into attractive spaces for artisans' studios and craft shops, collectively known as the Viaduc des Arts. The workshops house a wealth of creativity: furniture and tapestry restorers, interior designers, cabinet-makers, violin- and flute-makers, embroiderers and fashion and jewellery designers; a full list and map is available from no. 23 avenue Daumesnil.

The Bois de Vincennes

Daily dawn till dusk; follow signs from avenue Daumesnil (see p.164 and Paris map inside front cover) or take Métro line 1 to its terminus at Château de Vincennes. The Bois de Vincennes is one of the largest green spaces that the city has to offer. Sights are quite a long way from each other, so to avoid a lot of footslogging, target one or two or rent a bicycle from the outlet on Esplanade St-Louis (weekends & hols; €3 an hour) just south of Château de Vincennes.

The place to head for if you've only got a limited amount of time is the **Parc Floral** (daily: summer 9.30am–8pm, winter 9.30am–dusk. €1.50; Ⓦwww.parcfloraldeparis.com), Paris's best garden, a short walk southeast from the Château de Vincennes. Flowers are always in bloom in the Jardin des Quatre Saisons; you can picnic beneath pines, then wander through concentrations of camellias, rhododendrons, cacti, ferns, irises and bonsai trees. Between April and September, there are art and horticultural exhibitions in several pavilions, free jazz and classical music concerts, and numerous activities for children, including a mini-golf of Parisian monuments.

If you just feel like a lazy day out in the park, you could go boating on the **Lac Daumesnil**, near the Porte Dorée entrance and Métro station (line 8). In the southeast corner, off route de la Pyramide, you can wander among 2000 trees of over 800 different species that have been cultivated in the **Arboretum** (Mon–Fri 9.30am–6.30pm; free). Just north of the Lac Daumesnil, at 53 avenue de St-Maurice, is the city's largest **zoo** (April–Sept Mon–Sat 9am–6pm, Sun 9am–6.30pm; Oct–March closes one hour earlier. €8, children €5), one of the first to replace cages with trenches and use landscaping to give the animals room to exercise. The animals are at their most animated during the feeding times scheduled throughout the afternoon.

Château de Vincennes

Daily 10am–noon & 1.15–6pm. 75min guided tours at 11am, 2.15pm, 3pm & 4.45pm; 45min tours at 10.15am, 11.45am, 1.30pm & 4.15pm. €6.10 75min tour, €4.60 45min. On the northern edge of the *bois*, the Château de Vincennes – erstwhile royal medieval residence, then state prison, porcelain factory, weapons dump and military training school – is still undergoing restoration work started by Napoleon III. The fourteenth-century keep is closed but tours stop at another highlight – the Flamboyant-Gothic Chapelle Royale, completed in the mid-sixteenth century and decorated with superb Renaissance stained-glass windows.

Shops

Le Baron Rouge

1 rue Théophile-Roussel. Tues–Fri
10am–2pm & 5–9.30pm, Sat
10am–9.30pm, Sun 10.30am–1pm.
A wine-cellar and bar selling a
good selection of dependable
lower-range French wines at
modest prices.

Cécile et Jeanne

49 av Daumesnil. Mon–Fri
10am–7pm, Sat & Sun 2–7pm.
Reasonably priced and
innovative jewellery design in
one of the Viaduc des Arts
showrooms.

FNAC Musique

4 place de la Bastille ⓦwww.fnac.fr.
Mon–Sat 10am–8pm, Wed & Fri to
10pm. A stylish shop in black,
grey and chrome with
computerized catalogues, every
variety of music, books, and a
concert booking agency.

Isabel Marant

16 rue de Charonne. Mon–Sat
10.30am–7.30pm. Marant has
established an international
reputation for her feminine
and flattering clothes in quality
fabrics such as silk and
cashmere. Prices are above
average, but not exorbitant.

▼ LE BARON ROUGE

Cafés

Café de l'Industrie

16 rue St-Sabin. Daily 10am–2am.
One of the best Bastille cafés,
packed out every evening. Rugs
on the floor around solid old
wooden tables, mounted
rhinoceros heads, old black-and-
white photos on the walls and
an unpretentious crowd
enjoying the comfortable
absence of minimalism.

Café des Phares

7 place de la Bastille (west side). Daily
7am–4am. A popular public
philosophy debate is held in the
back room here every Sunday at
11am. At other times the *terrasse* is
a good spot for people-watching
on the place de la Bastille.

Pause Café

41 rue de Charonne, cnr rue Keller.
Tues–Sat 8am–2am, Sun to 9pm.
More like "Pose Café" – given
its popularity with the *quartier*'s
young and fashionable who
pack the pavement tables at
lunch and aperitif time.

Bars

Bar des Ferrailleurs

18 rue de Lappe. Daily 5pm–2am.
Dark and stylishly sinister, with
rusting metal decor, an
eccentric owner and a
relaxed and friendly
crowd.

SanZSanS

49 rue du Faubourg St-
Antoine. Daily 9am–2am.
Gothic decor of red
velvet, oil paintings
and chandeliers, and a
young crowd in the
evening. Drinks and
food reasonably priced.
DJ every evening.

Restaurants

Le Bistrot du Peintre

116 av Ledru-Rollin ☎01.47.00.34.39.
Mon–Sat 7am–2am, Sun 10am–8pm.
A charming, traditional *bistrot*,
where small tables are jammed
together beneath faded Art
Nouveau frescoes and wood
panelling. The emphasis is on
reasonably priced, hearty
Auvergne cuisine.

Blue Elephant

43–45 rue de la Roquette
☎01.47.00.42.00. Daily noon–2.30pm
& 7pm–midnight; closed Sat midday.
Superb, pricey Thai restaurant
with dishes featuring liberal
amounts of papaya, coconut milk
and seafood. Booking essential.

Bofinger

7 rue de la Bastille ☎01.42.72.87.82.
Mon–Fri noon–3pm & 6.30pm–1am,
Sat & Sun noon–1am. This popular
fin-de-siècle brasserie, with its
splendid, perfectly preserved,
original decor, is always
crowded with Bastille Opera-
goers and tourists. Specialities
are sauerkraut and seafood.
Prices above average.

Chez Paul

13 rue de Charonne, cnr rue de Lappe
☎01.47.00.34.57. Daily noon–2.30pm
& 7.30pm–12.30am; closed Aug. A
wonky corner building housing
a small restaurant that preserves
the faded colours and furnishings
of an older Bastille era, right
down to the black-and-white
tiles on the floor. The young
customers who pack the place
out, however, have a distinctly
contemporary style. Moderately
priced. Booking advised.

Le Square Trousseau

1 rue Antoine Vollon ☎01.43.43.06.00.
Tues–Sat noon–2pm & 7.30–midnight;
closed Aug. A handsome *belle
époque* brasserie serving
excellent, fair-priced traditional
cuisine. Booking recommended.

Live music

Café de la Danse

5 passage Louis-Philippe
☎01.47.00.57.59. Rock, pop,
world and folk music played in
an intimate and attractive space.

Opéra Bastille

120 rue de Lyon ☎08.36.69.78.68,
@www.opera-de-paris.fr. Operas
put on at the Bastille are often
on a grand scale and have a high
reputation – best to book in
advance. For programme and
booking details consult their
website or phone the box office.
Tickets can cost as little as €10
if you sit up in the gods, but
most are around the €60–90
mark.

Clubs

Chapelle des Lombards

19 rue de Lappe ☎01.43.57.24.24.
Thurs–Sat 11pm–dawn; entry and first
drink Thurs €13, Fri & Sat €18. This
erstwhile *bal musette* still plays
the occasional waltz and tango,
but for the most part the music
is Afro-Latin. Its renown as a
pick-up joint means unabashed
advances.

La Fabrique

53 rue du Faubourg St-Antoine
☎01.43.07.67.07. Mon–Sat
11pm–5am. Free Mon–Thurs, around
€10 Fri & Sat. Uber-trendy club-
bar heaving with Bastille
groovesters partying well into
the morning.

Eastern Paris

Traditionally a working-class area, with a history of radical and revolutionary activity, eastern Paris is nowadays one of the most diverse and vibrant parts of the city, home to sizeable ethnic populations, as well as students and impoverished artists, attracted by the area's low rents. The area's most popular attractions are **Père-Lachaise** cemetery, the final resting place of many well-known artists and writers; the **Canal St-Martin**, with its trendy cafés and bars; and the vast, postmodern **Parc de la Villette**. Visiting the **Parc de Belleville** and the bucolic **Parc des Buttes-Chaumont** reveals the east's other chief asset – near-panoramic views of the city.

The Canal St-Martin

Built in 1825 to enable river traffic to shortcut the great western loop of the Seine around Paris, the Canal St-Martin possesses a great deal of charm, especially along its southern reaches: plane trees line the cobbled *quais,* and elegant, high-arched footbridges punctuate the spaces between the locks, from where you can still watch the odd barge slowly rising or sinking to the next

▼ CANAL ST-MARTIN

level. In the last decade or so the area has been colonized by the new arty and media intelligentsia, and the bars, cafés and boutiques fronting the canal and in the surrounding streets have an alternative, bohemian feel. The area is particularly lively on Sunday afternoons when the *quais* are closed to traffic, and pedestrians, cyclists and rollerbladers take over the streets, and students hang out along the canal's edge, nursing beers or softly strumming guitars.

The Parc de la Villette

Daily 6am–1am. Grounds free, admission fee for some themed gardens. Ⓦwww.villette.com. Built in 1986 on the site of what was once Paris's largest abattoir and meat market, the Parc de la Villette's landscaped grounds include a state-of-the-art science museum, a superb music museum, a series of themed gardens and a number of jarring, bright-red "follies". The effect of these numerous, disparate elements can be quite disorienting – all in line with

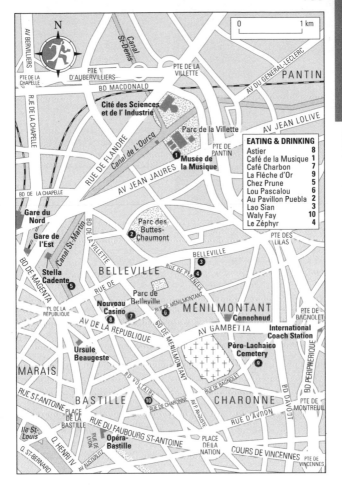

EATING & DRINKING

Astier	8
Café de la Musique	1
Café Charbon	7
La Flèche d'Or	9
Chez Prune	5
Lou Pascalou	6
Au Pavillon Puebla	2
Lao Sian	3
Waly Fay	10
Le Zéphyr	4

the creators' aim of eschewing meaning and "deconstructing" the whole into its parts. All very well, but on a practical level you'll probably want to pick up a map at the information centre at the southern entrance to help you make sense of it all.

The extensive park grounds contain ten themed gardens, aimed mainly at children. In the Jardin des Miroirs, for example, steel monoliths hidden amongst the trees and scrub cast strange reflections, while, predictably, dune-like shapes, sails and windmills make up the Jardin des Vents et des Dunes (for under-12s only and accompanying adults). Also popular with children is the eighty-metre-long Dragon Slide.

▲ CITE DES SCIENCES

In front of the Cité des Sciences floats the **Géode** (Tues–Sat hourly shows 10.30am–9.30pm, 10.30am–7.30pm; €8.75), a bubble of reflecting steel that looks as though it's been dropped from an intergalactic boules game into a pool of water. Inside is a screen for Omnimax films, not noted for their plots, but a great visual experience.

Cité des Sciences et de l'Industrie

Parc de la Villette ⓦwww.cite-sciences.fr. Tues–Sat 10am–6pm, Sun 10am–7pm. €7.50. Planetarium shows 11am, noon, 2pm, 3pm, 4pm & 5pm; 35min; €2.50. The Cité des Sciences et de l'Industrie is one of the world's finest science museums, set in a huge building, four times the size of the Pompidou Centre. Its giant walls are made of glass and the centre of the museum is left open to the full extent of the roof, 40m high. An excellent programme of temporary exhibitions complements the permanent exhibition, called **Explora**, covering

subjects such as sound, robotics, energy, light, ecology, maths, medicine, space and language. As the name suggests, the emphasis is on exploring, and there are numerous interactive computers, videos, holograms, animated models and games. You can have your head spun further by a session in the planetarium.

The Cité has a special section for children called the **Cité des Enfants**, with areas for 3- to 5-year-olds and 6- to 12-year-olds; all children have to be accompanied by an adult and you pay for a ninety-minute session consisting of organized activities as well as individual play (☏08.03.30.63.06. Tues, Thurs & Fri 11.30am, 1.30pm & 3.30pm; Wed, Sat, Sun & public hols 10.30am, 12.30pm, 2.30pm & 4.30pm). Among the numerous engaging activities, children can play about with water, construct buildings on a miniature construction site (complete with cranes, hard hats and barrows), experiment with sound and light, manipulate robots and superimpose their image on a landscape.

Musée de la Musique

Cité de la Musique complex, Parc de la Villette. Tues–Sat noon–6pm, Sun 10am–6pm. €6.10. The Musée de la Musique presents the history of music from the end of the Renaissance to the present day,

▼ CITE DE LA MUSIQUE

both visually, exhibiting some 4500 instruments, and aurally, via headsets (available in English; free). Glass case after glass case holds gleaming, beautiful instruments: jewel-inlaid crystal flutes and a fabulous lyre-guitar are some impressive examples. The instruments are presented in the context of a key work in the history of Western music: as you step past each case, the headphones are programmed to emit a short scholarly narration, followed by a delightful concert.

Père-Lachaise cemetery

Main entrance on boulevard de Ménilmontant. Mon–Fri 8am–5.30pm, Sat 8.30am–5.30pm, Sun 9am–5.30pm. Free. Final resting place of a host of French and foreign notables, Père-Lachaise covers some 116 acres, making it one of the world's largest cemeteries. Size aside, it's surely also one of the most atmospheric – an eerily beautiful haven, with terraced slopes and magnificent old trees that spread their branches over the moss-grown tombs. Free plans are given out at the entrance, though it's worth buying a slightly more detailed plan, as it's tricky tracking down some of the graves; the best is the one published by Editions Métropolitain Paris (around €2), usually available in the newsagents and florists near the main entrance.

Père-Lachaise was opened in 1804 to ease the strain on the city's overflowing cemeteries and churchyards. The civil authorities had Molière, La Fontaine, Abélard and Héloïse reburied here, and to be interred in Père-Lachaise quickly acquired cachet. Among the most visited graves is that of

▲ OSCAR WILDE'S GRAVE, PERE-LACHAISE

Chopin (Division 11), often attended by Poles bearing red-and-white wreaths and flowers. Fans also flock to the ex-Doors lead singer Jim Morrison (Division 6), who died in Paris at the age of 28. You can tell when you're getting near his grave: messages in praise of love and drugs are scribbled on nearby trees and tombs.

Femme fatale Colette's tomb, close to the main entrance in Division 4, is very plain, though always covered in flowers. The same holds true for Sarah Bernhardt's (Division 44) and the great *chanteuse* Edith Piaf's (Division 97). Marcel Proust lies in his family's black-marble, conventional tomb (Division 85).

Cutting a rather romantic figure, French president Félix Faure (Division 4), who died in the arms of his mistress in the Elysée palace in 1899, lies draped in a French flag, his head to one side. One of the most impressive of the individual tombs is Oscar Wilde's (Division 89), topped with a sculpture by Jacob Epstein of a mysterious Pharaonic winged messenger

▲ PARC DES BUTTES-CHAUMONT

(sadly vandalized of its once prominent member, last seen being used as a paper weight by the director of the cemetery).

It is the monuments to the collective, violent deaths, however, that have the power to change a sunny outing to Père-Lachaise into a much more sombre experience. In Division 97, you'll find the memorials to the victims of the Nazi concentration camps and executed Resistance fighters. Marking one of the bloodiest episodes in French history is the Mur des Fédérés (Division 76), the wall where the last troops of the Paris Commune were lined up and shot in the final days of the battle in 1871. The man who ordered their execution, Adolphe Thiers, lies in the centre of the cemetery in Division 55.

Parc des Buttes-Chaumont

The Parc des Buttes-Chaumont was constructed under Haussmann in the 1860s to camouflage what until then had been a desolate warren of disused quarries, rubbish dumps and shacks. Out of this rather unlikely setting, a fairy-tale-like park was created – there's a grotto with a cascade and artificial stalactities, and a picturesque lake from which a huge rock rises up, topped with a delicate Corinthian temple. From the temple you get fine views of the Sacré-Cœur and beyond, and you can also go boating on the lake.

Belleville

The neighbourhood of Belleville's colourful, if somewhat run-down, main street, rue de Belleville, abounds with Vietnamese, Thai and Chinese shops and restaurants, which spill south along boulevard de Belleville and rue du Faubourg-du-Temple. The *quartier's* rich ethnic mix is also evident on rue Ramponeau, which is just off boulevard de Belleville, and is full of kosher shops, belonging to Sephardic Jews from Tunisia. African and oriental fruits, spices, music and fabrics attract shoppers to the boulevard de Belleville market on Tuesday and Friday

▼ PARC DE BELLEVILLE

mornings. From the **Parc de Belleville**, with its terraces and waterfalls, you get fantastic views across the city, especially at sunset.

Ménilmontant

Like Belleville, Ménilmontant aligns itself along one straight, steep, long street, the rue de Ménilmontant and its lower extension rue Oberkampf. Although it is seedy and dilapidated in parts, its popularity with students and artists has brought a cutting-edge vitality to the area. Alternative shops and trendy bars and restaurants have sprung up among the grocers and cheap hardware stores, especially along rue Oberkampf.

Shops

Ganachaud

226 rue de Pyrénées. Tues–Sat 7.30am–8pm. Although father Ganachaud has left the business, his three daughters continue his recipes, and the bread is still out of this world. Start the day with a *pain biologique* and you'll live to be a hundred years, guaranteed.

Stella Cadente

93 quai de Valmy. 10am–7.30pm. Soft and feminine clothes, such as floaty chiffon dresses, from designer Stanislassia Klein.

Ursule Beaugeste

15 rue Oberkampf. Mon–Fri 11am–7.30pm, Sat 3–7pm. Designer Ann Grand Clément's delicious trademark crocheted handbags, some made on old looms, as well as beautifully engraved leather bags and cloth hats, all presented in a simple industrial-chic decor.

Cafés

Café de la Musique

213 av Jean-Jaurès. Daily 7am–2am. A stylish café with a popular terrace, just inside the La Villette complex.

Café Charbon

109 rue Oberkampf ☎01.43.57.55.13. Daily 9am–2am, DJ Thurs, Fri & Sat eves 10pm–2am, live music Sun from 8.30pm. A very successful and attractive resuscitation of an early twentieth-century café, popular with a young, fashionable crowd.

Restaurants

Astier

44 rue Jean-Pierre-Timbaud
℡01.43.57.16.35. Mon–Fri noon–2pm
& 8–11pm; closed Aug, plus a fortnight
in May & at Christmas. A popular
restaurant with simple decor,
unstuffy atmosphere, and food
renowned for its freshness and
refinement. Outstanding
selection of perfectly ripe
cheeses. Essential to book ahead;
lunch is often less crowded and
just as enjoyable. Prices are
reasonable.

Chez Prune

36 rue Beaurepaire ℡01.42.41.30.47.
Mon–Sat 7.30am–1.45am & Sun
10am–1.45am. One of the most
popular hangouts along the
canal, this is a very friendly,
inexpensive and laid-back bar-
restaurant. Creative *assiettes*
guaranteed to tempt both meat-
eaters and vegetarians, and a
romantic place to sip a glass of
wine or indulge in a dessert.

Au Pavillon Puebla

Parc des Buttes-Chaumont
℡01.42.08.92.62. Tues–Sat
noon–10pm; closed two weeks in
August. Luxury cuisine in an old
hunting lodge (enter by the rue
Botzaris/avenue Bolivar gate to
the park). Poached lobster and
duck with *foie gras* are some of
the *à la carte* delights. Not cheap,
but well worth the extra.

Waly Fay

6 rue Godefroy-Cavaignac,
℡01.40.24.17.79. Mon–Sat noon–2pm
& 7.30–11pm; closed last two weeks
of Aug. A West African restaurant
with a cosy, stylish atmosphere,
the dim lighting, rattan and old,
faded photographs creating an
intimate, faintly colonial
ambience. Smart, young black
and white Parisians come here
to dine on perfumed, richly
spiced stews and other West
African delicacies at a moderate
cost.

Le Zéphyr

1 rue Jourdain ℡01.46.36.65.81.
Mon–Sat 8am–11.30pm, closed Sat
lunch. Trendy but relaxed and
moderately priced 1930s-style
bistrot with an attractive
terrace.

Bars

Lou Pascalou

14 rue des Panoyaux. Daily 9am–2am.
Trendy but friendly place with a
zinc bar. Wide range of cocktails
and beers bottled and on tap.

La Flèche d'Or

102 bis rue de Bagnolet
℡01.43.72.04.23,
⊛www.flechedor.com. Daily
10am–2am. A large, lively café-bar
attracting the arty, biker, punkish
Parisian youth. It's also a nightly
venue for live world music, pop,
punk, ska and *chanson*, and the
reasonably priced food also has a
multicultural slant.

Clubs

Nouveau Casino

109 rue Oberkampf ℡01.43.57.57.40,
⊛www.nouveaucasino.net. Thurs–Sun
11pm–dawn. €10. Eclectic mix of
musical styles played at this
large, happening club – anything
from electro to house and funk.
Concerts earlier in the evening
are even wider-ranging – from
post-rock to hip-hop.

Western Paris

Commonly referred to as the **Beaux Quartiers**, Paris's well-manicured western arrondissements, the 16e and 17e, are the preserve of moneyed Parisians. The most appealing areas are the old villages of **Auteuil** and **Passy** at its heart, with their tight knot of streets and charming *villas* – leafy lanes of attractive old houses, fronted with English-style gardens of roses, ivy and wisteria. The 16e also boasts a number of interesting examples of early-twentieth-century architecture, notably pieces by Le Corbusier and Hector Guimard. Another highlight in the area is the **Musée Marmottan**, with its marvellous collection of late Monets. Just behind the museum lies the extensive **Bois de Boulogne**, an extremely pleasant spot with its trees, lakes, cycling trails and the beautiful floral displays of the **Parc de Bagatelle**. Further west, modern architecture comes bang up to date with the gleaming skyscrapers of the purpose-built commercial district of **La Défense**, dominated by the enormous **Grande Arche**.

Auteuil

Around Auteuil are several of Hector Guimard's Art Nouveau buildings – there's a concentration on rue de la Fontaine, the best-known at no. 14, Castel Béranger, with exuberant decoration and shapes in the windows, the roofline and the chimney. If the bulgy curves of Art Nouveau make you feel queasy, however, head up rue du Dr-Blanche for the cool, rectilinear lines of architect Le Corbusier's contribution to the area.

Villa La Roche

Square du Dr Blanche. Mon 1.30pm–6pm, Tues–Fri 10.30am–12.30pm & 1.30pm–6pm; closed Aug. €2.40. Le Corbusier's first private houses, dating to 1923, were the Villa Jeanneret and the Villa La Roche. This latter is in strictly Cubist style,

very plain, with windows in bands, the only extravagance a curved frontage. It may look commonplace enough now from the outside, but at the time it was built it was in great contrast to anything that had gone before, and once you're inside, the spatial play still seems groundbreaking. The interior is appropriately decorated with Cubist paintings.

Place de Passy

The heart of the Passy *quartier* is pleasant little place de Passy, with its crowded but leisurely *Le Paris Passy* café. Leading off from here is the old high street, rue de Passy, with its eye-catching parade of boutiques, and the cobbled, pedestrianized rue de l'Annonciation, an agreeable blend of genteel affluence and the down-to-earth.

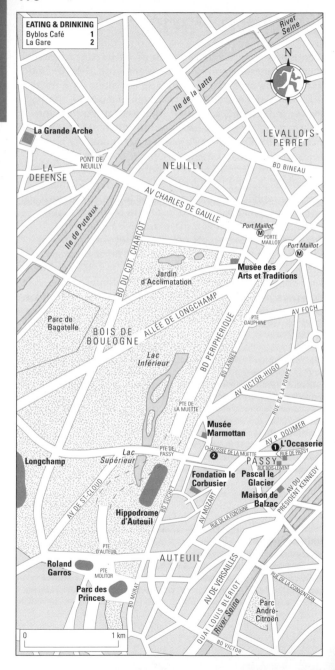

EATING & DRINKING

Byblos Café	1
La Gare	2

N

River Seine

Ile de la Jatte

La Grande Arche

LEVALLOIS-PERRET

LA DEFENSE

PONT DE NEUILLY

NEUILLY

BD BINEAU

AV CHARLES DE GAULLE

Ile de Puteaux

BD DU CDT CHARCOT

Port Maillot
PORTE MAILLOT

Port Maillot

Jardin d'Acclimatation

Musée des Arts et Traditions

Parc de Bagatelle

ALLÉE DE LONGCHAMP

PTE DAUPHINE

AV FOCH

BOIS DE BOULOGNE

BD PERIPHERIQUE

BD LANNES

Lac Inférieur

AV VICTOR-HUGO

RUE DE LA POMPE

PTE DE LA MUETTE

AV P. DOUMER

Musée Marmottan

L'Occaserie

Longchamp

Lac Supérieur

PTE DE PASSY

CHAUSSÉE DE LA MUETTE

RUE DE PASSY

PASSY

RUE BOIS-LE-VENT

AV DE ST-CLOUD

BD SUCHET

Fondation le Corbusier

Pascal le Glacier

AV DU PRÉSIDENT KENNEDY

Maison de Balzac

Hippodrome d'Auteuil

AV MOZART

RUE DE LA FONTAINE

PTE D'AUTEUIL

AUTEUIL

Roland Garros

PTE MOLITOR

Parc des Princes

BD MURAT

AV DE VERSAILLES

QUAI LOUIS BLÉRIOT

River Seine

RUE DE LA CONVENTION

Parc André-Citroën

BD VICTOR

0   1 km

The Musée Marmottan

2 rue Louis-Boilly
Ⓦwww.marmottan.com. Daily
10am–6pm. €6.50. The Musée
Marmottan is best known for its
excellent collection of Monet
paintings. One of the highlights
is *Impression, soleil levant*, a canvas
from 1872 of a misty Le Havre
morning, and whose title the
critics usurped to give the
Impressionist movement its
name. There's also a dazzling
selection of works from Monet's
last years at Giverny, including
several *Nymphéas* (Waterlilies),
Le Pont Japonais, *L'Allée des
Rosiers* and *Le Saule Pleureur*.
The collection also features
some of his contemporaries –
Manet, Renoir and Berthe
Morisot – and a room full of
beautiful medieval illuminated
manuscripts.

Maison de Balzac

47 rue Raynouard. Tues–Sun
10am–6pm. Free. The Maison de
Balzac is a wonderful, summery
little house with pale-green
shutters, tucked away down some
steps that lead through a shady,
rose-filled garden, a delightful
place to dally on wrought-iron
seats, surrounded by busts of the
writer. It was here that Balzac
wrote some of his best-known

▲ BOIS DE BOULOGNE

works, including *La Cousine Bette*
and *Le Cousin Pons*. The museum
preserves his study, while other
exhibits include a highly
complex family tree of around a
thousand of the four thousand-
plus characters that feature in his
Comédie Humaine.

Bois de Boulogne

The Bois de Boulogne was
designed by Baron Haussmann
and supposedly modelled on
London's Hyde Park – though it's
a very French interpretation. The
"bois" of the name is somewhat
deceptive, though the extensive
parklands (just under 900
hectares) do contain some
remnants of the once great Forêt
de Rouvray. As
its location
would suggest,
the Bois was
once the
playground of
the wealthy,
although it also
established a
reputation as the
site of the sex
trade and its
associated crime.
The same is true
today and you

▼ MAISON DE BALZAC

should avoid it at night. By day, however, the park is an extremely pleasant spot to stroll, especially in the Parc de Bagatelle.

The best, and wildest, part for walking is towards the southwest corner. Bikes are available for rent at the entrance to the Jardin d'Acclimatation adventure park and you can go boating on the Lac Inférieur. Also within the park is the fascinating Musée National des Arts et Traditions Populaires.

Parc de Bagatelle

Bois de Boulogne. Daily 9am–7pm. €1.50. The Parc de Bagatelle comprises a range of garden styles from French and English to Japanese. Its most famous feature is the stunning rose garden. The best time for the roses is June, while in other parts of the garden there are beautiful displays of tulips, hyacinths and daffodils in early April, irises in May, and waterlilies in early August.

The Jardin d'Acclimatation

Bois de Boulogne. Daily: June–Sept 10am–7pm; Oct–May 10am–6pm. €2.50, children €1.25, under-3s free; rides from €2.50. The children's Jardin d'Acclimatation is a cross between a funfair, zoo and amusement park. The fun starts at the Porte-Maillot Métro stop: a little train runs from here to the Jardin (every 15min 11am–6pm; €5 return, ticket combines return ride and entry to park). The park's attractions include bumper cars, donkey rides, sea lions, bears and monkeys, a huge trampoline and a magical mini-canal ride (la rivière enchantée). There are also two museums: the high-tech Exploradôme (daily 10am–6pm. €5), designed to help children discover science and art, and the

Musée en Herbe (Mon–Fri & Sun 10am–6pm, Sat 2–6pm), which aims to bring art history alive through workshops and games. Bikes are available for rent at the entrance.

Musée National des Arts et Traditions Populaires

Bois de Boulogne. 6 ave du Mahatma-Gandhi. Mon & Wed–Sun 9.30am–5.15pm. €4, Sun €2.60. The absorbing Musée National des Arts et Traditions Populaires is dedicated to French rural life over the last thousand years or so and celebrates the traditional crafts of, among others, boat-building, shepherding, weaving, pottery and stone-cutting as they existed before industrialization and mass production.

La Défense

An impressive complex of gleaming skyscrapers, La Défense is Paris's prestige business district and an extraordinary monument to late-twentieth-century capitalism. Its most popular attraction is the huge Grande

▲ GRANDE ARCHE DE LA DÉFENSE

Arche; between there and the river, apartment blocks and big businesses compete to dazzle and dizzy you. The jungle of concrete and glass is relieved by avant-garde sculptures by artists such as Joan Miró and Torricini, dotted around the place de la Défense and the esplanade du Général de Gaulle between the Arche and the river.

For the most dramatic approach to the Grande Arche and to see the sculptures, it's worth getting off the Métro a stop early, at Ⓜ Esplanade-de-la-Défense.

Grande Arche de la Défense

Lifts daily 10am–8pm. €7. The Grande Arche de la Défense, built in 1989 for the bicentenary of the Revolution, is a beautiful and astounding 112-metre-high structure, clad in white marble, standing 6km out and at a slight angle from the Arc de Triomphe, completing the western axis of this monumental east–west vista. Lifts take you up past a "cloud canopy" to the roof of the arch, from where on a clear day you can see as far as the Louvre and beyond.

Shops

L'Occaserie

30 rue de la Pompe. Tues–Sat 11am–7pm. Specialists in secondhand haute couture and a great hunting ground for Chanel suits, Louis Vuitton handbags and the like. While prices are much cheaper than new, they're still not especially inexpensive. There are several smaller branches nearby at 16 & 21 rue de l'Annonciation, 14 rue Jean-Bologne and 19 rue de la Pompe.

Pascal le Glacier

17 rue Bois-le-Vent. Tues–Sat 11am–6pm. Exquisite home-made sorbets in fruity flavours, such as sanguino orange and mango.

Restaurants

Byblos Café

6 rue Guichard ☎ 01.42.30.99.99 Daily 11am–3pm & 5–11pm. An excellent Lebanese restaurant, serving traditional mezzes, moussaka and the like in relaxed and convivial surroundings. Prices are very reasonable for the area.

La Gare

19 Chaussée de la Muette ☎ 01.42.15.15.31. Restaurant daily noon–3pm & 7pm–midnight, bar noon–2pm. This renovated train station is now an elegant restaurant-bar serving, among other things, a very popular, though slightly pricey, lunch menu. You can sit out on the attractive terrace on sunny days.

Excursions

Even if you're on a weekend break, a handful of major sights may tempt you beyond the city limits. Firstly there's the château de Versailles, the ultimate French royal palace, awesome in its size and magnificence. St-Denis, meanwhile, just beyond the city centre, is principally famous for its historic Gothic cathedral, the burial place of the kings of France. As for Disneyland Paris, 25km east of the capital, there are no two ways about it – children will love it. It offers a good variety of fear-and-thrill rides along with the Disney-themed spectacles, and it's easy to visit as a day-trip.

Château de Versailles

RER Line C to Versailles-Rive Gauche station. 40min trip. Signposted 10min walk from the station. Tues–Sun except hols: May–Sept 9am–6pm; Oct–April 9am–5pm. €20 "passport", individual tickets also available. ⊛www.chateauversailles.fr. In the early 1660s, the "Sun King" Louis XIV recruited the elite design team of the day – architect Le Vau, painter Le Brun and gardener Le Nôtre – and set them to create a palace that would be the apotheosis of French royal indulgence. Work lasted virtually until Louis XIV's death in 1715. Rather than a royal home, Versailles was the headquarters and lodgings of every arm of the state, and the entire court of some 3500 nobles – plus administrative staff, soldiers, merchants and servants – lived in the palace, in a state of unhygienic squalor, according to contemporary accounts. For the nobility, every minute of the day revolved around the actions of the king,

▼ VERSAILLES

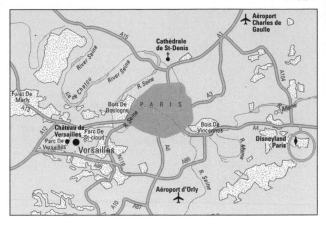

which were minutely regulated and rigidly encased in ceremony.

Following Louis' death, the château mostly remained the residence of the royal family until the Revolution of 1789, when the furniture was auctioned off and the pictures dispatched to the Louvre – a process that took a year. Restoration only began in earnest between the two world wars, but today it proceeds apace, Versailles' curators scouring the world's auction houses in search of the original furnishings from the eve of the Revolution. The palace's main **entrances** lie beyond the giant gates, past the equestrian statue of Louis XIV, in the glorious, half-enclosed Cour de Marbre. The door marked "A", often signalled by long queues, gives access to the main showcase rooms of the palace, the **State Apartments**, which can be visited without a guide (€7.50, or €5.30 after 3.30pm). The route leads past the royal chapel, a grand structure that ranks among France's finest

Baroque creations, and through a procession of gilded drawing rooms to the king's throne room and the dazzling Galerie des Glaces, or Hall of Mirrors, which runs in one chandelier-strewn, mirrored sweep along the length of the garden front. It's best viewed at the end of the day, when the crowds have departed and the setting sun floods it from the west. The queen's fabulous apartments line the northern wing, beginning with her bedchamber, restored exactly as it was in its last refit of 1787, with hardly a surface unadorned by gold leaf. A separate entrance in the Cour de Marbre, marked "D", is the place to book the excellent **guided tours** (€4–8), which take you to wings of the palace that mostly can't otherwise be seen (though a few are covered by "self-guided" tours using audio-visual guides). Various itineraries depart throughout the day, including English-language tours; they must all be booked the same morning, so arrive early.

▲ GALERIE DES GLACES, VERSAILLES

Versailles park

Daily 7am–dusk: €3. Le Nôtre's
exquisite, statue-studded garden
terraces lie between the
château and the landscaped part
of the park. In the summer
months, the fountains here
dance elaborately to the tune of
classical music (July–Sept Sat &
Sun 11am, 3.30pm & 5.20pm;
April–June Sat only; €6).
Beyond the gardens, the slope
falls away to the grand canal
and the "English" park, which
is big enough to spend the
whole day exploring, along
with its lesser outcrops of royal
building mania: the Italianate
Grand Trianon, designed by
Hardouin-Mansart in 1687 as a
"country retreat" for Louis
XIV; and the exquisite **Petit
Trianon** (daily: April–Oct
noon–6pm; Nov–March
noon–5pm; combined ticket
for both Trianons €5, or €3
after 3.30pm), built in the
1760s for Louis XV's mistress,
Mme de Pompadour, as a
refreshingly elegant change of
scene from the over-
indulgences of the palace.

Just beyond these is the bizarre
Hameau de la Reine, a full-
scale play village and thatch-
roofed farm built in 1783 for
Marie-Antoinette to indulge the
fashionable, Rousseau-inspired
fantasy of returning to the
natural life. Around it, the park
is being slowly returned to its
original design from the time of
Marie-Antoinette, which means
some areas may be fenced off
for re-landscaping.

Distances in the park are
considerable but all the sights
are well signposted. If you want
to save time walking, take the
petit train, which shuttles
between the terrace in front of
the château and the Trianons
(€3.50); it runs about every
15min in summer. There are
bikes for hire at the Grille de la
Reine, Porte St-Antoine and by
the Grand Canal. Boats are for
hire on the Grand Canal, next
to a pair of **café-restaurants** –
picnics are forbidden.

The basilica of St-Denis

St-Denis-Basilique Métro, end of line
13. April–Sept Mon–Sat
10am–6.15pm, Sun noon–6.15pm;
Oct–March Mon–Sat 10am–5.15pm,
Sun noon–5pm. Free; tombs €6.10.
The basilica of St-Denis is often
called the birthplace of Gothic
architecture. It's a typically lofty,
serene space, but melancholy
too – as the burial place of
almost all of the kings of
France. The church gets its
name from its legendary
founder, the early Parisian
bishop St Denis - who was
decapitated for his beliefs at
Montmartre but promptly
picked up his own head and
walked all the way to St Denis –
but the present basilica was
begun only in the first half of
the twelfth century by Abbot
Suger, friend and adviser to
kings. Only the lowest storey of
the choir remains from this era,

as much of the rest of the church was rebuilt in the Rayonnant Gothic style in the mid-thirteenth century. The abbey's royal connections date back to the coronation of Pepin the Short, in 754, but it wasn't until Hugh Capet, in 996, that it became the royal necropolis. Since then, all but three of France's kings have been interred here. Their very fine **tombs**, often graced by startlingly naturalistic effigies, are distributed about the transepts and ambulatory (closed during services). Among the most interesting are the enormous Renaissance memorial to François I on the right just beyond the entrance, and the tombs of Louis XII, Henri II and Catherine de Médicis on the left side of the church. On the level above – invariably graced by bouquets of flowers – are the undistinguished statues of Louis XVI and Marie-Antoinette.

St-Denis market

St-Denis-Basilique Métro, end of line 13. You probably wouldn't make a special trip out to St-Denis from the centre of Paris, but if you're here visiting the basilica it's well worth exploring the area around. Modern St-Denis is the most infamous of Paris's "hot" suburbs, previously for its radically Communist population, now for its supposedly volatile ethnic mix. In fact, it's a fascinating place to visit, characterized by the extraordinary, fortress-like architecture of its shopping and housing complexes. Try to time your visit to coincide with market day (Tues, Fri & Sun mornings), when the main place Victor-Hugo is crammed with shoppers.

▼ THE BASILICA OF ST-DENIS

Visiting Disneyland Paris

RER line A to Marne-la-Vallée/Chessy station. 40min trip. Park hours roughly: April–Oct daily 9am to 11pm; Nov–March daily 10am to 8pm. ⓦ www.disneylandparis.com

The Disneyland complex is divided into three areas: **Disneyland Park**; **Walt Disney Studios Park**; and **Disney Village** and the hotels. If you plan to stay here, booking an accommodation-and-entry package through Disney or a travel agent offers the best value for money.

The best **time to go** is on an off-season weekday (Mon & Thurs are best). At other times, longish waits for the popular rides are common in the middle of the day. The most popular attractions use the Fastpass scheme, where you book yourself a later time slot at the entrance to the ride and go on some less popular rides while you wait.

Passes, known as "passports", can be purchased in advance – in order to avoid queues at the park itself – at the Paris Tourist Office and at all Disney shops, or you can buy admission passes and train tickets in Paris at all RER line A and B stations and in major Métro stations. You can also buy tickets online. The one-day pass (April–Sept €39, under-11s €29; Oct–March except over Christmas €29, under-11s €25) allows you to visit either Disneyland Park or the Walt Disney Studios Park. You can't go back and forth between both areas, but if you choose the Walt Disney Studios, you're entitled to move on to Disneyland Park after the Studios close. Otherwise, you're allowed re-entry. If you buy the three-day pass (April–Sept €107, under-11s €80; Oct–March €79, under-11s kids €69) you can move freely between both areas, and you don't have to use the ticket on three consecutive days.

There are licensed cafés inside the park but expect the usual captive-audience prices and quality; the swankier restaurants in Disney Village aren't great value, but the various hamburger joints around the park aren't too pricey.

Disneyland Park

The introduction to Disneyland Park is **Main Street USA**, a mythical vision of a 1900s American town, that leads up to **Central Plaza**, the hub of the park. A steam train **Railroad** runs round the park with stations at each "land" and at the main entrance. Sleeping Beauty's Castle, directly opposite Main Street across Central Plaza, belongs to **Fantasyland**, which is aimed at the youngest children. There are no height restrictions here, and rides are mostly gentle. Each of the other three themed areas offers a landmark rollercoaster and a theme: **Adventureland** has the most outlandish, jungly sets, **Frontierland** is set in the Wild West, while **Discoveryland**

emphasizes technology and the space age. As for rollercoasters, the runaway train on Frontierland's Big Thunder Mountain and the mine-carts of Adventureland's Indiana Jones and the Temple of Peril: Backwards! are fast and exciting, but the emphasis is on thrills rather than sheer terror. Space Mountain, in Discoveryland, is a different matter altogether: the upside-down loops, corkscrews and terrifying acceleration require you to have a strong constitution to enjoy it really. Be warned that the experience can be so intense that the park's gentler rides may seem disappointing. Children, in particular, will want to return again and again.

Walt Disney Studios Park

Other than the "Rock 'n' Roller Coaster Starring Aerosmith", a terrifyingly fast, corkscrew-looping, Metal-playing white-knuckler, the new Walt Disney Studios Park complex lacks the big rides offered by its older, larger neighbour. In some ways it's a more satisfying affair, focusing on what Disney was and is still renowned for – animation. You can try your hand at drawing, there are mock film and TV sets where you can be part of the audience, and the special-effects and stunt shows are impressive in their way. The Studio Tram Tour Featuring Catastrophe Canyon is more of a true ride, taking you past various fake film lots and pausing inside the accident-prone Catastrophe Canyon. The Armageddon Special Effects spaceship simulation is also pretty scary, while it lasts.

▲ DISNEYLAND PARIS

Accommodation

Accommodation

Hotels

Paris is extremely well supplied with hotels. The ones reviewed here are all classics, places that offer something special – whether it's a great location, unusually elegant decor or a particularly warm welcome. Some are sights in themselves. The grandest establishments are mostly found in the Champs-Elysées area, while the trendy Marais quarter is a good bet for something elegant but relatively relaxed. Over on the Left Bank – around the Quartier Latin, St-Germain and the Eiffel Tower quarter – you'll find more homely, old-fashioned hotels.

Most hotels offer two categories of rooms: at the bottom end of the scale this means choosing between an en-suite bathroom or shared facilities, while more expensive places may charge a premium rate for larger or more luxurious rooms. Overseas visitors may find that prices aren't exorbitant, by European standards, but then rooms can be surprisingly small for the money.

Continental **breakfast** is normally an extra €5 to €8 per person; you'll usually be asked if you want to have breakfast when you check in.

The Islands

Henri IV 25 place Dauphine ☎01.43.54.44.53 ⓜ Pont Neuf/Cité. See map on p.190. A well-known cheapie in a beautiful central location on the Ile de la Cité. Ask for one of the recently renovated en-suite rooms (€43); most of the others are pretty run-down and have only a *cabinet de toilette*. Essential to book well in advance. No credit cards. €30–43.

Hôtel du Jeu de Paume 54 rue St-Louis-en-l'Île ☎01.43.26.14.26, ⓦwww.jeu depaumehotel.com ⓜ Pont-Marie. See map on p.190. Located on the most desirable island in France, this quiet, charming hotel occupies the site of a tennis court built for Louis XIII in 1634 ("jeu de paume" is "real tennis"). The wood-beam court is now a breakfast room, from which a glass lift whisks you up to the 28 rooms, decorated in soothing colours. €215–€285.

The Champs-Elysées and Tulleries

Hôtel d'Artois 94 rue la Boétie ☎01.43.59.84.12, ☎01.43.59.50.70 ⓜ St-Phillipe-du-Roule. See map on p.192. One of the cheapest in this, the smartest part of town, with spacious doubles of the old-fashioned variety. €52–€75.

Hôtel Le Bristol 112 rue du Faubourg St-Honoré ☎01.53.43.43.00, ⓦwww.le bristolparis.com ⓜ Miromesnil. See map on p.192. The city's most luxurious hotel

Booking accommodation

It's wise to **reserve** your accommodation as early as possible, as the nicest places are quickly booked out for all but the quietest winter months. All receptionists speak some English – but it's worth bearing in mind that more and more places offer **online** booking as well. If you book by phone you may be asked for just a credit card number, or sometimes for written or faxed confirmation. If you're stuck, the main tourist office at Champs Elysées and the branches at Gare de Lyon and the Eiffel Tower will find you a room: all book accommodation for that day only, and you have to turn up at the office in person (€3–8 commission for a hotel room depending on how many stars it has, €1.20 for a hostel).

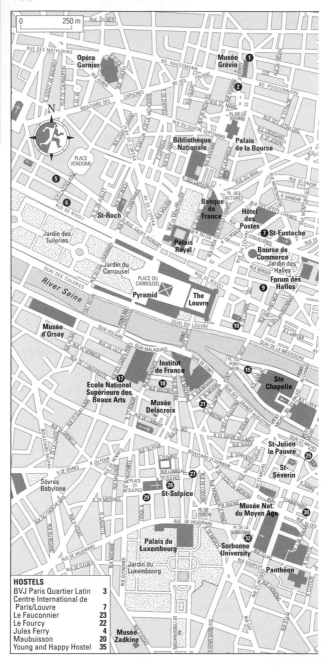

HOSTELS

BVJ Paris Quartier Latin	3
Centre International de Paris/Louvre	7
Le Fauconnier	23
Le Fourcy	22
Jules Ferry	4
Maubuisson	20
Young and Happy Hostel	35

HOTELS

Familia Hôtel	33	Hôtel Chopin	1	Hôtel Pavillon		
Grand Hôtel Jeanne d'Arc	14	Hôtel Costes	5	de la Reine	12	
Grand Hôtel du Loiret	13	Hôtel Esmeralda	25	Hôtel Récamier	29	
Grand Hôtel Malher	19	Hôtel Gilden-Magenta	3	Hôtel du Septième Art	24	
Hôtel de l'Angleterre	17	Hôtel du Globe	27	Hôtel de la Sorbonne	32	
Hôtel Beaumarchais	8	Hôtel des Grandes Écoles	34	Hôtel St-Honore	9	
Hôtel Brighton	6	Hôtel Henri IV	15	Hôtel Vivienne	2	
Hôtel Caron de		Hôtel du Jue de Paume	26	L'Hôtel	18	
Beaumarchais	16	Hôtel Marignan	30	Relais du Louvre	10	
Hôtel Central Marais	11	Hôtel de Nesle	21	Relais Saint-Sulpice	28	

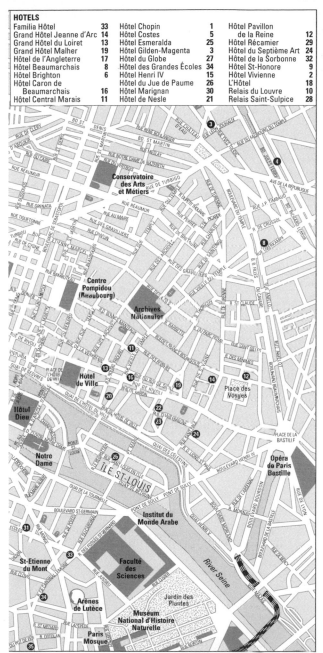

manages to remain discreet and warm. Gobelins tapestries adorn the walls and some rooms have private roof gardens. There's also a large colonnaded interior garden, as well as a swimming pool, health club and gourmet restaurant. Doubles start at €580.

Hôtel Keppler 12 rue Keppler ☎01.47 .20.65.05, ⓦwww.hotelkeppler.com ⓂGeorge V/Kléber. **See map below.** Located in a quiet street just a few steps from the Arc de Triomphe, this place is good value for the area. Rooms are a little small, but spotless and quite comfortable. Doubles €84–88.

Hôtel Lancaster 7 rue de Berri ☎01.40 .76.40.76, ⓦwww.hotel-lancaster.fr ⓂGeorge V. **See map below.** An elegantly

restored nineteenth-century town house with 58 rooms, each retaining original features and antiques, but with a touch of contemporary chic. A small interior zen-style garden and pleasant service make for a relaxing stay. Doubles start at €410.

Hôtel Brighton 218 rue de Rivoli ☎01.47 .03.61.61,ⓔhotel.brighton@wanadoo.fr ⓂTuileries. **See map on p.190.** A smart establishment with light, airy rooms. Its main asset, though, is the magnificent view of the Tuileries gardens from the front-facing rooms – the ones right at the top with balcony are the best. Rates range from €138 (double, no view) to €252 (triple, with view).

Hôtel Costes 239 rue St-Honoré ☎01.42 .44.50.00, ⓕ01.42.44.50.01 ⓂTuileries. **See map on p.190.** Opened in the mid-

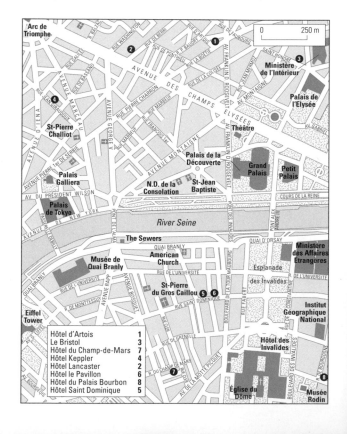

Hôtel d'Artois	1
Le Bristol	3
Hôtel du Champ-de-Mars	7
Hôtel Keppler	4
Hôtel Lancaster	2
Hôtel le Pavillon	6
Hôtel du Palais Bourbon	8
Hôtel Saint Dominique	5

1990s and an instant hit with media and fashion celebrities, this ultra-cool modern hotel marries Second Empire style with all up-to-date amenities. Doubles start from €300.

The Grands Boulevards and passages

Hôtel Chopin 46 passage Jouffroy; entrance on bd Montmartre, near rue du Faubourg-Montmartre ☎01.47.70.58.10, ℱ01.42.47.00.70 Ⓜ Grandes-Boulevards. See map on p.190. A charming, quiet hotel in a splendid period building hidden away at the end of an elegant 1850s *passage*. Rooms are pleasantly furnished. €70–82.

Hôtel Vivienne 40 rue Vivienne ☎01.42.33.13.26, Ⓔparis@hotel-vivienne.com Ⓜ Grandes-Boulevards. See map on p.190. Ideally located for the Opéra Garnier and the Grands Boulevards, this is a friendly hotel, with good-sized, fresh, clean rooms. €65–€90.

Beaubourg and Les Halles

Relais du Louvre 19 rue des Prêtres St-Germain l'Auxerrois ☎01.40.41.96.42, Ⓔau-relais-du-louvre@dial.deane.com Ⓜ Palais-Royal/Musée-du-Louvre. See map on p.190. Small, discreet hotel done out in Second Empire style. Its relaxed atmosphere and charming service attract a faithful clientele. €145–180.

Hôtel St-Honoré 85 rue St-Honoré ☎01.42.36.20.38, Ⓔhotel-st-honore@wanadoo.fr Ⓜ Châtelet Les Halles. See map on p.190. Conveniently close to the heart of things, this is a stylishly renovated old building with 29 rooms, all en suite. €74.

The Marais

Hôtel Caron de Beaumarchais 12 rue Vieille-du-Temple ☎01.42.72.34.12, Ⓦwww.carondebeaumarchais.com

Ⓜ Hôtel-de-Ville. See map on p.190. Named after the eighteenth-century French playwright Beaumarchais, who lived just up the road, this gem of a hotel has only nineteen rooms. Everything – down to the original engravings and Louis XVI-style furniture, not to mention the pianoforte in the foyer – evokes the refined tastes of high-society pre-Revolutionary Paris. Rooms overlooking the courtyard are small but cosy (€120–137), while those on the street are more spacious, some with balcony (€152).

Hôtel Central Marais 33 rue Vieille-du-Temple ☎01.48.87.56.08, Ⓦwww.hotelcentralmarais.com Ⓜ Hôtel-de-Ville. See map on p.190. The only self-proclaimed gay hotel in Paris, with a relaxed bar downstairs. Seven small rooms with shared bathrooms (€87). Also lets an apartment that sleeps four (€110, three nights minimum). The entrance is on rue Ste-Croix-de-la-Bretonnerie.

Grand Hôtel Jeanne d'Arc 3 rue de Jarente ☎01.48.87.62.11, Ⓦwww.hotel jeannedarc.com Ⓜ St-Paul. See map on p.190. An attractive old Marais building, just off place du Marché Ste-Catherine. The rooms are a decent size, with nice individual touches, plus cable TV. The triple at the top has good views over the rooftops (€108). Doubles cost €78.

Grand Hôtel du Loiret 8 rue des Mauvais-Garçons ☎01.48.87.77.00, Ⓔhotelloiret@aol.com Ⓜ Hôtel-de-Ville. See map on p.190. A friendly, good value hotel, renovated in 2002. The two triples on the top floor have excellent views of the Sacré-Cœur. Cheaper rooms have wash-basin only, but all have TV and telephone. €35–€60.

Grand Hôtel Malher 5 rue Malher ☎01.42.72.60.92, Ⓦwww.grandhotel malher.com Ⓜ St-Paul. See map on p.190. A family-run establishment, situated right in the heart of the Marais. Rooms are light and well decorated, with gleaming-white bathrooms. Breakfast is served in a renovated seventeenth-century vaulted wine cellar. €107.

Hôtel Pavillon de la Reine 28 pl des Vosges, ☎01.40.29.19.19, Ⓦwww.pavillon-de-la-reine.com Ⓜ Bastille. See map on p.190. A perfect honeymoon or romantic-weekend getaway in a beautiful ivy-covered mansion secreted away off the place des Vosges. Rooms are sumptuously decorated with rich fabrics, antique furnishings and four-poster beds and come with all mod cons. Doubles start at €335.

Hôtel du Septième Art 20 rue St-Paul, ℡01.44.54.85.00, ✆hotel7art @wanadoo.fr Ⓜ St-Paul/Sully Morland. See map on p.190. A pleasant, comfortable place decorated with posters and photos from old movies; a similarly themed *salon de thé* downstairs. The stairs and bathrooms live up to the black-and-white-movie style. Doubles range from €70 to €120.

The Quartier Latin

Familia Hôtel 11 rue des Écoles ℡01.43.54.55.27, ✆www.hotel-paris -familia.com Ⓜ Cardinal-Lemoine. See map on p.190. Friendly, family-run hotel in the heart of the *quartier*. Rooms are small but characterful, with beams, elegant wallpaper and pretty murals. Some top-floor rooms have views of Notre-Dame, while a few more expensive ones have balconies. Double rooms cost €90–110, breakfast included.

Hôtel Esmeralda 4 rue St-Julien-le-Pauvre ℡01.43.54.19.20, ✆01.40.51 .00.68 Ⓜ St-Michel. See map on p.190. Nestling in an ancient house on square Viviani, this discreet, old-fashioned hotel has cosy, unmodernized rooms, some with superb views of nearby Notre-Dame. A trio of singles (€35) come with washbasin only; doubles cost €85.

Hôtel des Grandes Écoles 75 rue du Cardinal-Lemoine ℡01.43.26.79.23, ✆www.hotel-grandes-ecoles.com Ⓜ Cardinal-Lemoine. See map on p.190. This pretty three-star in the heart of the Quartier Latin has an attractive setting around a peaceful courtyard garden. Rooms are attractively bright, if rather heavy on the floral wallpaper, and cost €100–125, depending on size.

Hôtel Marignan 13 rue du Sommerard ℡01.43.54.63.81, ✆www.hotel -marignan.com Ⓜ Maubert-Mutualité. See map on p.190. The Marignan is totally

sympathetic to the needs of backpack-toting foreigners, with free laundry facilities, a dining room with fridge and microwave and bedrooms for up to five people. Even if you don't have a backpack, you'll find it central and welcoming – one of the best bargains in town. Doubles cost €60 with shared bathroom, or €82 en suite.

Hôtel Port-Royal 8 bd Port-Royal ℡01.43.31.70.06, ✆www.portroyal hotel.fr.st Ⓜ Gobelins. See map on p.148. The rooms at this excellent budget address wouldn't disgrace a three-star. It's immaculately clean, attractive and friendly, though towards the southern edge of the quarter. Fifteen inexpensive rooms (€48) are available with shared bathroom facilities, though showers cost €2.50. En-suite doubles cost €73.

Hôtel de la Sorbonne 6 rue Victor-Cousin ℡01.43.54.58.08, ✆www.hotel sorbonne.com Ⓜ Cluny-La Sorbonne. See map on p.190. Housed in an attractive old building almost on top of the Sorbonne, and close to the Luxembourg gardens, this is a small, quiet and rather plush hotel. Expect to pay around €80 for a double.

St-Germain

L'Hôtel 13 rue des Beaux-Arts ℡01.44 .41.99.00 ✆www.l-hotel.com Ⓜ Mabillon/St-Germain-des-Prés. See map on p.190. This extravagant four-star is a destination in itself, with a celebrity clientele and prices climbing above the €300 mark – notably for the room Oscar Wilde died in. The twenty sumptuously decorated, almost kitsch rooms are set round a light-well-like central atrium, and there's a tiny pool underground.

Hôtel de l'Angleterre 44 rue Jacob ℡01.42.60.34.72, ✆anglotel@wanadoo.fr Ⓜ St-Germain-des-Prés. See map on p.190. Top-class hotel in a building that once housed the British Embassy and, later, Ernest Hemingway. The luxury rooms (€230) are huge, and many have beautiful original roof beams. Standard room prices begin at €130.

Hôtel du Globe 15 rue des Quatre-Vents ℡01.43.26.35.50, ✆01.46.33.62.69, Ⓜ Odéon. See map on p.190. Welcoming hotel in a tall, narrow, seventeenth-century building decked out with a faintly medieval theme: there are four-posters, stone walls, roof beams and even a suit of armour in the lobby. Doubles cost from €90.

Hôtel de Nesle 7 rue de Nesle
℡01.43.54.62.41, Ⓜ St-Michel.
Ⓦwww.hoteldenesle.com. See map on p.190. Friendly, offbeat hotel with themed rooms decorated with wacky cartoon murals – of French history, mostly – that you'll either love or hate. Smaller rooms cost €75, some of which have shared bathrooms and one of which even has a hammam. En-suite rooms are €100.

Hôtel Récamier 3 bis place St-Sulpice
℡01.43.26.04.89, Ⓟ01.46.33.27.73,
Ⓜ St-Sulpice. See map on p.190.
Comfortable, old-fashioned and solidly bourgeois hotel, attractively tucked away in a corner behind St-Sulpice. Double rooms cost from €115.

Relais Saint-Sulpice 3 rue Garancière
℡01.46.33.99.00, Ⓦhttp://monsite
.wanadoo.fr/relaisstsulpice, Ⓜ St-Sulpice.
See map on p.190. Set in an aristocratic town house immediately behind St Sulpice, this is a discreet and classy three-star. The well-furnished rooms are painted in cheerful Provençal colours and cost €165 for a standard or €205 for a luxury room.

Eiffel Tower area

Hôtel du Champ-de-Mars 7 rue du Champs-de-Mars ℡01.45.51.52.30,
Ⓦwww.hotel-du-champ-de-mars.com,
Ⓜ Ecole-Militaire. See map on p.192. A friendly and well-run hotel just off the rue Cler market. The rooms are decidedly cosy, with swathes of colourful fabrics. Doubles from €74.

Hôtel du Palais Bourbon 49 rue de Bourgogne ℡01.44.11.30.70, Ⓦwww
.hotel-palais-bourbon.com, Ⓜ Varenne.
See map on p.192. This handsome old hotel on a sunny street by the Musée Rodin offers spacious and light double rooms at €120, plus one tiny double at €55.
Breakfast is included.

Hôtel le Pavillon 54 rue St-Dominique
℡01.45.51.42.87, Ⓔpatrickpavillon
@aol.com, Ⓜ Invalides/La Tour Maubourg.
See map on p.192. A tiny former convent set back from the tempting shops of the rue St-Dominique. Rooms are small and very simple, but good value in this area at €78; the spacious family rooms cost €100.

Hôtel Saint Dominique 62 rue Saint-Dominique ℡01.47.05.51.44, Ⓦwww
.hotelstdominique.com, Ⓜ Invalides/La Tour Maubourg. See map on p.192. The posh, village-like neighbourhood of the rue St-Dominique is the perfect setting for this welcoming two-star. The prettily wallpapered rooms are arranged around a bright little courtyard. Rooms cost around €120.

Montparnasse

Hôtel Istria 29 rue Campagne-Première
℡01.43.20.91.82, Ⓔhotel.istria
@wanadoo.fr, Ⓜ Raspail. See map on p.143. Beautifully decorated hotel, with legendary artistic associations: Duchamp, Man Ray, Aragon, Mayakovsky and Rilke all stayed here. Doubles from €96.

Hôtel des Voyageurs 22 rue Boulard
℡01.43.21.08.20, Ⓔhotel.des
.voyageurs2@wanadoo.fr, Ⓜ Denfert Rochereau. See map on p.143. A truly original, great value, Montparnasse establishment, with temporary art exhibitions lining the walls and theatre events taking place in the garden at the back. The rooms are comfortable and modern, and guests can use the kitchen and living room. The new annexe on adjacent rue Daguerre has free unlimited Internet access in every room, and every wall and door surface has been frescoed by local artists. €45.

Southern Paris

Hôtel Printemps 31 rue du Commerce
℡01.45.79.83.36, Ⓔhotel.printemps
.15e@yahoo.fr, Ⓜ Avenue Emil Zola. See map on p.148. A friendly welcome and rooms that are sparsely furnished but clean. Popular with backpackers. €39 for the room, whether used by one or two people, plus some inexpensive rooms with just sinks and loos for €30.

Hôtel Tolbiac 122 rue de Tolbiac
℡01.44.24.25.54, Ⓦwww.hotel
-tolbiac.com, Ⓜ Tolbiac. See map on p.148. Situated on a noisy junction, but all

rooms are clean and decently furnished, and very inexpensive – doubles cost from €29, or €36 with bathroom facilities. In July and August you can rent small studios by the week.

Résidence Les Gobelins 9 rue des Gobelins ☎01.47.07.26.90, ⓦwww.hotel gobelins.com, ⓜ Gobelins. See map on p.148. A delightful establishment within walking distance of the Quartier Latin's rue Mouffetard. With its large, comfortable double rooms at €70, this is a well-known bargain, so book well in advance.

Montmartre and northern Paris

Hôtel Bonséjour 11 rue Burq ☎01.42.54.22.53, ⓕ01.42.54.25.92, ⓜ Abbesses. See map on p.154. Set in a marvellous location on a quiet, untouristy street, this hotel is run by friendly and conscientious owners, and the rooms, which are basic, but clean and spacious, are Montmartre's best deal. Corner rooms 23, 33, 43 and 53 have a balcony and a €2 supplement. Doubles cost €30 with shared shower facilities, otherwise €40. Three-person rooms also available.

Hôtel le Bouquet de Montmartre 1 rue Durantin ☎01.46.06.87.54, ⓦwww .bouquet-de-montmartre.com, ⓜ Jules-Joffrin. See map on p.154. The decor is rather overwhelmingly floral, but the rooms are comfortable and very good value at €65, and the location on the corner of lively place des Abbesses is excellent.

Hôtel Ermitage 24 rue Lamarck ☎01.42 .64.79.22, ⓜ Anvers. See map on p.154. A discreet, welcoming, family-run hotel, hidden away behind Sacré-Cœur. Rooms are slightly chintzy in the classic French manner, and the ones at the back have views out across northern Paris. Approach via the funicular to avoid a steep climb. Doubles cost €86, breakfast included.

Hôtel Langlou/des Croisés 63 rue St-Lazare. ☎01.48.74.78.24, ⓔhotel-des -croises@wanadoo.fr. , 150m east of ⓜ Trinité. See map on p.154. Superbly genteel hotel that's hardly changed in half a century, with a beautiful old lift and unusu-

ally large rooms. Doubles cost €89–99, depending on size.

Style Hôtel 8 rue Ganneron. From ⓜ Place-de-Clichy head 250m north up Ave de Clichy and turn right onto rue Ganneron; the hotel is just round the corner. ☎01.45.22.37.59, ⓕ01.45 .22.81.03, ⓜPlace-de-Clichy. See map on p.154. Wooden floors, marble fireplaces, a secluded internal courtyard, and nice people. Great value, especially in the rooms with shared bathrooms (€34). No lift. En-suite doubles cost €43, or €55 with three beds.

Timhotel Montmartre place Émile-Goudeau, 11 rue Ravignan ☎01.42 .55.74.79, ⓦwww.timhotel.com, ⓜ Abbesses. See map on p.154. Rooms are modern, comfortable and freshly decorated, albeit in a nondescript way. The location is classic, with views across the city from the more expensive (€145) rooms. €130.

The Bastille

Hôtel Bastille Speria 1 rue de la Bastille ☎01.42.72.04.01, ⓦwww.hotel-bastille -speria.com, ⓜ Bastille. See map on p.163. Located just off the place de la Bastille, this is a quiet, clean, comfortable place, en suite throughout, and run by helpful and pleasant staff. €106.

Hôtel Méridional 36 bd Richard-Lenoir ☎01.48.05.75.00, ⓕ01.43.57.42.85, ⓜ Brégeu Sabin. See map on p.163. A welcoming and attractive three-star on a fairly quiet road, handily located for the Marais and Bastille. Rooms are equipped with minibar, TV and Internet point and are attractively furnished in light oak and pastel colours. €130.

Eastern Paris

Hôtel Beaumarchais 3 rue Oberkampf ☎01.53.36.86.86, ⓕ01.43.38.32.86, ⓦwww.hotelbeaumarchais.com, ⓜ Filles-du-Calvaire. See map on p.190. A fashionable, funky hotel with personal service and colourful 1950s-inspired decor; all 31 rooms are en suite with air conditioning, safes and cable TV and cost from €99.

Hôtel Gilden-Magenta 35 rue Yves-Toudic ☎01.42.40.17.72, ⓦwww .multi-micro.com/hotel.gilden.magenta,

Ⓜ **République. See map on p.190.** A friendly hotel, with fresh, colourful decor; rooms 61 and 62, up in the attic, are the best and have views of the Canal St-Martin. Breakfast is served in a pleasant patio area. Doubles €69.

Hostels

Hostels are an obvious choice for a tight budget, but you won't necessarily save money on sharing a room in a budget hotel. Many now take advance bookings, including all three main hostel groups: FUAJ (Ⓦwww.fuaj.fr), which is part of Hostelling International; UCRIF (Ⓦwww.ucrif.asso.fr), which caters largely to groups; and MIJE (Ⓦwww.mije.com), which runs three excellent hostels in historic buildings in the Marais district, all of which need to be booked long in advance. You don't need to be a member to book – just join when you arrive. Independent hostels tend to be noisier, more youth-oriented places, often with bars attached. Hostels usually have a maximum stay of around a week, and there is often a curfew at around 2am, though some offer keys or door codes. Except where indicated below, there is no effective age limit.

BVJ Paris Quartier Latin 44 rue des Bernardins ⓣ01.43.29.34.80, Ⓦwww.bvjhotel.com, Ⓜ **Maubert-Mutualité. See map on p.190.** Typically institutional UCRIF hostel, but spick and span and in a good location. Dorm beds (€25), plus single or double rooms (€30/27 per person).

Centre International de Paris/Louvre 20 rue Jean-Jacques-Rousseau ⓣ01.53.00.90.90, Ⓦwww.bvjhotel.com, Ⓜ **Louvre/Châtelet-Les-Halles. See map on p.190.** A clean, modern and efficiently

run hostel for 18- to 35-year-olds. Book up to ten days in advance. Accommodation ranges from singles to eight-bed dorms. From €18.30 per person.

Le Fauconnier 11 rue du Fauconnier ⓣ01.42.74.23.45, Ⓕ01.40.27.81.64, Ⓜ **St-Paul/Pont Marie. See map on p.190.** MIJE hostel in a superbly renovated seventeenth-century building. Dorms (€27 per person) sleep three to eight, and there are some single (€42) and double rooms too (€32 per person), with en-suite showers.

Le Fourcy 6 rue de Fourcy ⓣ01.42.74.23.45, Ⓜ **St Paul. See map on p.190.** Another MIJE hostel housed in a beautiful mansion, this one has a small garden and an inexpensive restaurant. Dorms cost €27 per person, and there are some doubles (€32 per person with shower) and triples (€28 per person) too.

Jules Ferry 8 bd Jules-Ferry ⓣ01.43.57.55.60, Ⓦwww.fuaj.fr, Ⓜ **République. See map on p.154.** Fairly central HI hostel, in a lively area at the foot of the Belleville hill. Difficult to get a place, but they can help find a bed elsewhere. Only two to four people in each room; beds cost €19.

Maubuisson 12 rue des Barres ⓣ01.42.74.23.45, Ⓜ **Pont Marie/Hôtel de Ville. See map on p.190.** A MIJE hostel in a magnificent medieval building on a quiet street. Shared use of the restaurant at *Le Fourcy* (see above). Dorms only, sleeping four (€27 per person).

Woodstock Hostel 48 rue Rodier ⓣ01.48.78.87.76, Ⓦwww.woodstock.fr, Ⓜ **Anvers/St Georges. See map on p.154.** A well-run, friendly hostel in the *Three Ducks* stable, with its own bar. Set in a great location on a pretty street not far from Montmartre. Twin rooms available (€22). Book ahead.

Young and Happy Hostel 80 rue Mouffetard ⓣ01.45.35.09.53, Ⓦwww.youngandhappy.fr, Ⓜ **Monge/Censar-Daubenton. See map on p.190.** Noisy, basic and studenty independent hostel in a lively, if a tad touristy, position. Dorms, with shower, sleep four (€20 per person), and there are a few doubles (€25 per person). Curfew at 2am.

Essentials

Arrival

It's easy to get from both of Paris's main airports to the city centre using the efficient public transport links. The budget airline airport, Beauvais, is served by buses. If you're arriving by train, of course, it's easier still: just get on the Métro.

By air

The two main Paris **airports** that deal with international flights are Roissy-Charles de Gaulle and Orly, both well connected to the centre. Information on them can be found on ✪ www.adp.fr. A third airport, Beauvais, is used by some of the low-cost airlines. Bear in mind that you can buy a **Paris visite** card at the airports which will cover multiple journeys to and within the city (see p.203).

Roissy-Charles de Gaulle Airport

Roissy-Charles de Gaulle Airport (24hr information in English ☎ 01.48.62.22.80), usually referred to as Charles de Gaulle and abbreviated to CDG or Paris CDG, is 23km northeast of the city. The airport has two main terminals, CDG 1 and CDG 2, linked by a shuttle bus – when you leave, make sure you check which terminal your flight departs from.

There are various ways of getting to the centre of Paris, but the simplest is the **Roissyrail** train link which runs on RER line B and takes **30 minutes** (every 15min 5am–midnight; €7.75 one way). You can pick it up direct at CDG 2, but from CDG 1 you have to get a shuttle bus (*navette*) to the RER station first. The train is fast to the Gare du Nord, then stops at Châtelet-Les Halles, St-Michel and Denfert-Rochereau, all of which have Métro stations for onward travel.

Various **bus companies** provide services from the airport direct to various city-centre locations, but they're slightly more expensive than Roissyrail, and may take longer. A more useful alternative is the Blue Vans door-to-door **minibus** service (€14.50 per head if there are two or

more people, €22 for a single person; no extra charge for luggage; 6am–7.30pm). Bookings must be made at least 48 hours in advance on ☎ 01.30.11.13.00, by fax (℻ 01.30.11.13.09) or via their website ✪ www.airportshuttle.fr.

Taxis into central Paris from CDG cost around €35 on the meter, plus a small luggage supplement (€0.90 per item), and should take between fifty minutes and one hour. Note that if your flight gets in after midnight your only means of transport is a taxi.

Orly Airport

Orly Airport (information in English daily 6am–11.30pm ☎ 01.49.75.15.15), 14km south of Paris, has two terminals, Orly Sud (south; for international flights) and Orly Ouest (west; for domestic flights), linked by shuttle bus but easily walkable.

The easiest way into the centre is the **Orlyval**, a fast train shuttle link to RER station Antony, from where you can pick up RER line B trains to the central RER/Métro stations Denfert-Rochereau, St-Michel and Châtelet-Les Halles; it runs every four to eight minutes Monday to Saturday from 6.30am to 11pm, from 7am Sundays and holidays (€8.80 one way; 35min to Châtelet). Another service connecting with the RER is the Orlyrail bus–rail link: a shuttle bus takes you to RER line C station Pont de Rungis, from where the Orlyrail train leaves every twenty minutes from 5.50am to 10.50pm for the Gare d'Austerlitz and other Métro connection stops (€5.25 one way; train 35min, total journey around 50min). Leaving Paris, the train runs from Gare d'Austerlitz from 5.50am to 11.50pm.

Taxis take about 35 minutes to reach the centre of Paris and cost at least €20.

Beauvais Airport

Beauvais Airport (☎ 08.92.68.20.66, ✪ www.aeroportbeauvais.com) is a fair distance from Paris – some 65km north-

ESSENTIALS · City transport

west – and is used by some budget airlines. Coaches (€20 return) shuttle between the airport and Porte Maillot, at the northwestern edge of Paris, where you can pick up Métro line 1 to the centre. Coaches take about an hour, and leave between fifteen and thirty minutes after the flight has arrived and about three hours before the flight departs on the way back. Tickets can be bought at Arrivals or from the Beauvais shop at 1 boulevard Pershing, near the Porte Maillot terminal.

By rail

Eurostar (☎08.36.35.35.39, ⊕www.eurostar.com) trains terminate at the **Gare du Nord**, rue Dunkerque, in the northeast of the city – a bustling convergence of international, long-distance and suburban trains, the Métro and several bus routes. Coming off the train, turn left for the Métro and the RER, immediately right and through the side door for taxis (roughly €10 to the centre). The Eurostar offices and check-in point for departures are both located on the mezzanine level, above the main station entrance.

Gare du Nord is also the arrival point for trains from Calais and northern European countries such as Belgium, Germany and the Netherlands. Paris has five other mainline train stations, part of the national SNCF network: the **Gare de l'Est** (place du 11-Novembre-1918) serves eastern France and central and eastern Europe; the **Gare St-Lazare** (place du Havre), serves the Normandy coast and Dieppe, the **Gare de Lyon** (place Louis-Armand) serves Italy, Switzerland and TGV trains to southeast France. South of the river, the **Gare Montparnasse** (bd de Vaugirard) is the terminus for Chartres, Brittany, the Atlantic coast and TGV lines to southwest France and the Loire Valley; the **Gare d'Austerlitz** (bd de l'Hôpital) serves ordinary trains to the Loire Valley and the Dordogne. The motorail station, **Gare de Paris-Bercy**, is down the tracks from the Gare de Lyon on boulevard de Bercy.

For **information** on national train services and reservations phone ☎08.36.35.35.39 (if you dial extension 2 you should go through to an English-speaking operator) or consult the website ⊕www.sncf.fr. For information on suburban lines call ☎01.53.90.20.20. You can buy **tickets** at any train station, at travel agents and online at the SNCF website.

By road

If you're arriving by bus – international or domestic – you'll almost certainly arrive at the main **gare routière** at 28 av du Général-de-Gaulle, Bagnolet, at the eastern edge of the city; Métro Gallieni (line 3) links it to the centre. If you're **driving** in yourself, don't try to go straight across the city to your destination. Use the ring road – the **boulevard périphérique** – to get around to the nearest *porte*: it's much quicker (sometimes frighteningly so), except at rush hour, and far easier to navigate.

City transport

While walking is undoubtedly the best way to discover Paris, the city's integrated public transport system of bus, Métro and trains – RATP – is quick, inexpensive and efficient. Even the Batobus along the river comes under part of the same network. Taxis are surprisingly thin on the ground.

RATP

For 24-hour recorded information in English on all RATP services call ☎08.92.68.41.14 (premium rate) or visit ⊕www.ratp.fr.

Tickets and passes

The standard RATP **ticket** (€1.30 one way) is valid for any one-way Métro, bus or RER express rail ride anywhere within the city limits and immediate suburbs (zones 1 and 2). Only one ticket is ever needed on the Métro system, but you can't switch between buses or between bus and Métro/RER on the same ticket. For a short stay in the city, consider buying a reduced-price **carnet** of ten tickets (€10). All tickets are available from stations and *tabacs* (newsagent/tobacconist) – don't buy from the illegal touts. **Children** under 4 travel free, and kids aged 4 to 10 pay half price. Officially, you're supposed to keep your ticket until the end of the journey but you only actually need it to get through the entrance gates.

If you're travelling beyond the city limits (zones 3–5), to La Défense, for example, note that you'll need a separate **RER ticket**. Night buses (Noctambus) require separate tickets costing €2.50 each (buy these on board), unless you have a weekly or monthly travel pass (see below)

Mobilis day passes (€5.20) give unlimited access to the Métro, buses and RER trains within the city limits (zones 1 and 2). If you've arrived early in the week and are staying a few days, it might be more economical to buy the **Carte Orange weekly** coupon (€14.50 for zones 1 and 2) which is valid for an unlimited number of journeys from Monday morning to Sunday evening; you can buy it at all Métro stations and *tabacs* up until the Wednesday – you'll need a passport photo. On the Métro you put the Carte Orange coupon through the turnstile slot (make sure you retrieve it afterwards); on a bus you show the whole *carte* to the driver as you board – don't put it into the punching machine.

Paris Visite cards can be good value if bought at the airport when you arrive as they cover all travel within the city limits plus the airport rail links, Versailles and Disneyland Paris, as well as offering minor reductions on a few more touristy attractions. They cost €8.35, €13.70, €18.25 and €26.65 for one, two, three and five days respectively, and can begin on any day. A half-price child's version is also available. You can buy these passes from Métro stations and tourist offices or, if you're travelling to Paris by Eurostar, at

the information point in the departure lounge area of Waterloo International.

The Métro and RER

The **Métro**, combined with the **RER** suburban express lines, is the simplest way of moving around the city. Both run from around 5.30am to roughly 12.30am. Lines are colour-coded and designated by numbers for the Métro and letters for the RER. Platforms are signposted using the name of the terminus station; travelling north from Montparnasse to Châtelet, for example, you need to follow the signs for "Direction Porte-de-Clignancourt", at the northernmost end of the line. For RER journeys beyond the city, make sure that the station you want is illuminated on the platform display board. Free **maps** are available at most stations.

Stations (abbreviated: Ⓜ Concorde, RER Luxembourg, and so on) are evenly spaced and usually very close together, though interchanges can involve a lot of legwork. Many lines simply shadow the boulevards above.

Buses

Buses are often neglected in favour of the Métro but can be very useful where the Métro journey doesn't quite work. Every bus stop displays the numbers of the buses that stop there and a map showing all the stops on the route. Free **route maps** are available from Métro stations. Generally speaking, buses run from 6.30am to 8.30pm with a reduced service continuing to 1.30am; around half the lines don't operate on Sundays and holidays. **Night buses** (Noctambus) run on eighteen routes every hour (extra services on weekends) from 1am to 5.30am. **Tickets** (€1.30) are interchangeable with Métro tickets, and can be bought from the driver; make sure you put your ticket in the little stamping machine at the entrance to validate it.

Some bus routes are particularly good for **sightseeing**, notably bus #20 (the only one that's **wheelchair** accessible); bus #29, which has an open platform at the back; bus #24, along the Left Bank; and bus #73, down the Voie Triomphale.

Taxis

The best place to get a taxi is at one of the **taxi ranks** found at major junctions or railway stations (*arrêt taxi*) – usually more effective than trying to hail one from the street. Taxis can be any colour but carry distinctive roof lights – the large white light signals the taxi is free; the orange light means it's in use. You can also call a taxi out: **phone numbers** are shown at the taxi ranks, or try Taxis Bleus (℡08.91.70.10.10, Alpha Taxis (℡01.45 .85.85.85) or Artaxi (℡01.42.03.50.50). That said, finding a taxi at lunchtime and any time after 7pm can be almost impossible.

Charges – always metered – are fairly reasonable: between €6.50 and €11 for a central daytime journey, though considerably more if you call one out. Different day/night and city/suburb rates apply per kilometre, and there's a minimum charge of €5, a time charge of around €20 an hour for when the car is stationary, an extra charge of €0.75 if you're picked up from a mainline train station, and a €0.90 charge for each piece of luggage carried. A discretionary ten percent **tip** is usual. Taxi drivers do not have to take more than **three passengers** (they don't like people sitting in the front); if a fourth passenger is accepted, an extra charge of €2.50 will be added.

Batobus

A pleasant alternative to road and rail, the **Batobus** boat shuttle (✆www .batobus.com) operates from April to October stopping at eight points along the Seine in the following order: Port de la Bourdonnais (Ⓜ Eiffel Tower/Tro- cadéro), quai de Solférino (Ⓜ Assemblée Nationale), quai Malaquais (Ⓜ St-Ger- main-des-Prés), quai de Montebello (Ⓜ Notre-Dame), quai St Bernard (Jardin des Plantes), quai de l'Hôtel de Ville (Ⓜ Hôtel de Ville/Centre-Pompidou), quai du Louvre (Ⓜ Musée du Louvre) and Port des Champs-Elysées (Champs-Elysées). Boats run every 25 minutes from 10am to 9pm (until 7pm only in April, May and October). The total journey time is around 30 minutes, and tickets cost €2.50 for the first stop, €2.50 for subsequent stops, €10 for a day pass or €12.50 for a two-day pass.

Cycling

Cycling in Paris is as scary as you'd expect in a capital city, and there are lots of awkward one-way streets to find your way around. That said, you can almost always find a quiet back route, and the town hall has made great efforts to intro- duce cycle lanes. You can pick up a free leaflet, **Paris à Vélo**, outlining the routes, from town halls, the tourist office or bike rental outlets.

Between May and September, a num- ber of the roads along the Seine (the *quais*) are closed off on Sundays and public holidays (10am–6pm). They're popular places for cyclists and in-line skaters to meet up. The right bank of the Seine is freed of traffic from the Tuileries to Trocadéro, in the west, and from the Pont d'Austerlitz to the edge of the city, in the east; over on the Left Bank the roads are shut off from the Musée d'Orsay to the western side of the city. The *quais* along the Canal St-Martin are also closed on Sundays (2–6pm).

Prices for **bike rental** usually range from about €15–20 a day.

Bike 'n' Roller 38 rue Fabert ℡01.45.50.38.27, ✆www.bikenroller.fr (Ⓜ Invalides). Also rents out rollerblades. Daily 10am–7pm.

Paris À Vélo C'est Sympa 37 bd Bourdon ℡01.48.87.60.01, ✆www.paris velosympa.com (Ⓜ Bastille). One of the least expensive (from €24 for the week- end). Also does excellent three-hour bike tours of Paris (€30). Daily 9am–7pm, closed weekdays 1–2pm.

Paris-Vélo 2 rue du Fer-à-Moulin ℡01.43.37.59.22 (Ⓜ Censier-Dauben- ton). 21-speed and mountain bikes. Mon–Sat 10am–12.30pm & 2–7pm.

RATP/Maison Roue Libre 1 passage Mondétour ℡01.48.15.28.88 (Ⓜ Eti- enne-Marcel/Les Halles). RATP, the public bus- and Métro-operating company, rents out bikes from this site, open daily 9am–7pm. On weekends between March and October, RATP also hires out bikes from "cyclobuses" parked at the Bois de Vincennes and Bois de Boulogne bus stations; on Sundays, another cyclobus parks at 4 ave Victoria, on place du Châtelet (ⓂChâtelet).

Information

The main Paris **tourist office** is at 127 av des Champs-Elysées (daily 9am–8pm, except Oct–March Sun 11am–7pm; ☎08.92.68.31.12, ✉www.paris-touristoffice .com; ⓂCharles-de-Gaulle–Etoile). There are branch offices at the Gare de Lyon (Mon–Sat 8am–8pm), the Eiffel Tower (May–Sept daily 11am–6.40pm) and at 2 rue Auber, near the Opéra Garnier (Mon–Sat 9am–6.30pm). They give out information on Paris and the suburbs, can book hotel accommodation for you, and they also sell the Carte Musées et Monuments (see p.206), travel passes and phone cards. It's also worth picking up the free *Paris Map* – this might be behind the counter, so you'll need to ask.

Alternative sources of information are the **Hôtel de Ville information office** – Bureau d'Accueil – at 29 rue de Rivoli (Mon–Sat 9am–6pm; ☎01.42.76.43.43, ✉www.paris-france.org; ⓂHôtel de Ville), and the **Espace du Tourisme d'Île de France**, within the Carrousel du Louvre, underground below the triumphal arch at the east end of the Tuileries (daily except Tues 10am–7pm; ☎ 01.44 .50.19.98), which has information on attractions and activities in Paris and the surrounding area.

For detailed what's-on information it's worth buying one of Paris's inexpensive weekly **listings magazines** from a newsagent or kiosk. The best and glossiest is *Zurban* (✉www.zurban.com), though *Pariscope* (✉www.pariscope.com) has a comprehensive section on films and an English-language endpage section put together by *Time Out*. For more detail, French speakers should check out the monthly *Nova* magazine, while the free monthly magazine *Paris Voice* (✉www.parisvoice.com), available online and from English-language bookshops, has good listings as well as ads for flats and courses. Good nightlife listings are available at ✉www.parissi.com.

The **maps** in this guide and the free *Paris Map* (see above) should be adequate for a short sightseeing stay, but for a more detailed map your best bet is one of the pocket-sized "L'indispensable" series booklets, sold everywhere in Paris. The Michelin 1:10,000 *Plan de Paris* is comprehensive but unwieldy; more convenient are the *Rough Guide Map: Paris*, produced on waterproof, crease-resistant paper, and the *Falkplan*, which folds out only as you need it.

Museums and monuments

Entrance tickets to **museums and monuments** can really add up, though the permanent collections at all municipal museums are **free** all year round, while all national museums (including the Louvre, Musée d'Orsay and Pompidou Centre) are free on the first Sunday of the month – see ✉www.rmn.fr for a full list.

Each institution has its own policy for **children** and **teenagers**. In many museums under-18s go free, while all monuments are free for under-12s. Under-4s almost always get free admission. Half-price or reduced admission is normally available for 5- to 18-year-olds and students, though some commercial attractions charge adult rates from 12. The ISIC Card (International Student Identity Card; ⓦwww.isiccard.com) is usually the only card accepted for reduced-price **student** admission – often around a third off. For those **over 60 or 65**, depending on the institution (regardless of whether you are still working or not), reductions are often available; you'll need to carry your passport around with you as proof of age.

If you are going to do a lot of museum duty, consider buying the **Carte Musées et Monuments** (€15 one day, €30 three day, €45 five day). Available from the tourist office, RER/Métro stations and museums, as well as the Eurostar terminal at London Waterloo, it's valid for seventy museums and monuments in and around Paris, and allows you to bypass ticket queues.

Festivals and events

Paris hosts an impressive roster of festivals and events. Arguably the city's biggest jamboree is Bastille Day on July 14 but there's invariably something on to add extra colour to your stay.

Foire du Trône

Funfairs make a regular appearance in the capital, one of the most popular being the Foire du Trône (ⓦwww.foiredu trone.com), held in April and May in the Parc de Reuilly in the Bois de Vincennes (Porte Dorée entrance).

Fête de la Musique

On June 21, the Fête de la Musique (ⓦwww.fetedelamusique.culture.fr), buskers take to the streets and free concerts are held across the whole city in a fun day of music making.

Gay Pride

Gay and Lesbian Pride march (ⓦwww .gaypride.fr) on the last Saturday of June. A flamboyant parade of floats and costumes makes its way to the Bastille, followed by partying and club events with top DJs.

Bastille Day

On Bastille Day, July 14, the city celebrates the 1789 storming of the Bastille. The party starts the evening before with dancing around place de la Bastille; in the morning is the military march-past down the Champs-Elysées followed by fireworks.

Tour de France

On the third or fourth Sunday of July, Paris stages the final romp home of the Tour de France and thousands line the route to cheer the cyclists to the finish line on the Champs-Elysées.

Paris Plage

Paris Plage ("Paris Beach") is the transformation of part of the Seine into a "beach" from mid-July to mid-August, complete with real sand, deckchairs and palm trees.

Festival d'Automne

Running from the last week of September until Christmas, the Festival d'Automne (ⓦwww.festival-automne.com), is an international festival of theatre and music, much of it avant-garde and exciting.

Nuit Blanche

Nuit Blanche (ⓦwww.paris.fr), held in early October, is a night-long festival of poetry readings, concerts and performance art held in galleries, bars, restaurants and public buildings across the city.

Public holidays

France celebrates thirteen national holidays: January 1; Easter Sunday; Easter Monday; Ascension Day; Whitsun; Whit Monday; May 1; May 8; July 14; August 15; November 1; November 11; December 25. May is particularly festive.

Directory

ADDRESSES Paris is divided into twenty districts, or arrondissements. The first arrondissement, or "1er" is centred on the Louvre, in the heart of the city. The rest wind outward in a clockwise direction like a snail's shell: the 2e, 3e and 4e are central; the 5e, 6e and 7e lie on the inner part of the left (south) bank; while the 8e–20e make up the outer districts. Parisian addresses always quote the arrondissement, along with the nearest Métro station or stations, too.

BANKS AND EXCHANGE On the whole, the best exchange rates are offered by banks, though there's always a commission charge on top. Be very wary of bureaux de change, which cluster round arrival points and tourist spots, as they can really rip you off. Standard banking hours are Monday to Friday from 9am to 4 or 5pm. Some banks close for lunch; some are open on Saturday 9am to noon; all are closed on Sunday and public holidays. Money-exchange bureaux stay open until 6 or 7pm, tend not to close for lunch and may even open on Sundays in the more touristy areas.

BATEAUX MOUCHES Tourist boats operating on The Seine are known in general as "bateaux mouches", operators include: Bateaux-Mouches Information ☎01.40 .76.99.99, reservations ☎01.42.25 .96.10 ⊛www bateaux-mouches.fr. ⓂAlma-Marceau. Departs from the Embarcadère du Pont de l'Alma on the Right Bank. Rides last an hour. High-season departures 10am–11pm every 20 to 30 mins, low season confirmed departures 11am, 2.30pm, 4pm, 6pm and 9pm. Adults €7, children and seniors €4. Bateaux Parisiens ☎01.43.26.92.55 ⊛www.bateauxparisiens.com Ⓜ St-Michel. Departs from Port de la Bourdonnais on the Left Bank near the Eiffel Tower. High season departures every 30 mins 10am–11pm, low season every 30 mins 1pm–5pm & 8–10pm and every hour 10am–1pm & 5pm–8pm.

CINEMAS Paris has a world-renowned concentration of cinemas and moviegoers can chose from around three hundred films showing in any one week. Tickets rarely need to be purchased in advance and are good-value at around €8. *Le Grand Rex* 1 bd Poissonnière ⓂBonne Nouvelle. Famously kitsch Art-Deco cinema showing blockbusters (usually dubbed). *Max Linder Panorama* 24 bd Poissonnière Ⓜ Bonne Nouvelle. Opposite *Le Grand Rex*, this 1930s cinema shows films in the original format and has state-of-the-art sound. *La Pagode* 57 bis rue de Babylone Ⓜ François-Xavier. The most beautiful of the city's cinemas, *La Pagode* is a superb reproduction of a Japanese pagoda. *Reflet Medicis Logos, Quartier Latin* and *Le Champo* 3 rue Champollion, 9 rue Champollion and 51 rue des Ecoles Ⓜ Cluny-La-Sorbonne/Odéon. A cluster of inventive little cinemas offering up rare screening and classics.

CRIME Petty theft sometimes occurs on the Métro, at train stations and at tourist hotspots such as Les Halles and around rue de la Huchette, in the Quartier Latin. Serious crime against tourists is rare. The Préfecture de Police de Paris, for reporting thefts, is at 7 boulevard du Palais (☎01.53.73.53.73). For rape crisis (*SOS Viol*) call ☎08.00.05.95.95

DISABLED TRAVELLERS Paris has no special reputation for providing ease of access or facilities for disabled travellers. The way cars park on pavements makes wheelchair travel a nightmare, and the Métro system has endless flights of steps. Museums, however, are getting much better. Up-to-date information is best obtained from organizations at home before you leave, or the French tourist board (⊛www.franceguide.com)

EMBASSIES AND CONSULATES Australia, 4 rue Jean-Rey, 15e ☎01.40 .59.33.00, ⊛www.austgov.fr (Mº Bir-Hakeim); **Canada,** 35 av Montaigne, 8e ☎01.44.43.29.00, ⊛www.amb-canada.fr (ⓂFranklin-D-Roosevelt); **Ireland,** 4 rue

Rude, 16e ☎01.44.17.67.00 (Ⓜ Charles-de-Gaulle-Etoile); **New Zealand**, 7 rue Léonard-de-Vinci, 16e ☎01.45.00.24.11 (Ⓜ Victor-Hugo); **UK**, 35 rue du Faubourg St-Honoré, 8e ☎01.44.51.31.00, 🌐 www.amb-grandebretagne.fr (Ⓜ Concorde); **US**, 2 rue St-Florentin, 1er ☎01.43.12.22.22, 🌐 www.amb-usa.fr (Ⓜ Concorde).

EMERGENCIES Ambulance ☎15; police ☎17; fire ☎18.

GAY AND LESBIAN TRAVELLERS Paris has a vibrant, upfront gay community, and full-on prejudice or hostility is rare. Legally, France is liberal as regards homosexuality, with legal consent starting at 16 and laws protecting gay couples' rights. Useful contacts and listings can be found in the excellent glossy monthly magazine, Têtu (🌐 www.tetu .com), or online at 🌐 www.france tourism.com/gayguide/index.asp.

HEALTH Pharmacies can give good advice on minor complaints, offer appropriate medicines and recommend a doctor. British citizens with form E111 (from post offices) can take advantage of French health services. Non-EU citizens are strongly advised to take out travel insurance.

INTERNET Internet access is everywhere in Paris – if it's not in your hotel there'll likely be a café close by, and there are lots of *points internet* around the city centre. Most post offices, too, have a computer geared up for public Internet access.

MONEY All **ATMs** – *distributeurs* or *points argent*, found everywhere – give instructions in French or English. You can also use credit cards for (interest-paying) cash advances at banks and in ATMs, though some cards are rejected by French machines, which are set up to read the little golden chip on the front rather than the magnetic strip on the back – if this happens, just try another machine. When paying for things with a credit or debit card, you may be presented with a keypad and asked to tap in your PIN rather than sign a receipt.

POST French post offices (*la Poste*) – look for bright yellow-and-blue signs – are generally open Mon–Fri 8am–7pm,

Sat 8am–noon. However, Paris's main office, at 52 rue du Louvre, 1er (Ⓜ Etienne-Marcel), is open 24 hours for all postal services (but not banking). The easiest place to buy ordinary **stamps** (*timbres*) is at a *tabac* (tobacconist). Postcards (*cartes postales*) and letters (*lettres*) up to 20g cost €0.50 for the UK and EU, and €90 for North America, Asia and Oceania. For anything heavier, most post offices now have yellow-coloured *guichet automatiques* that weigh your letter or package and give you the correct stamps.

RACISM Paris has an unfortunate reputation for racism, but harassment of tourists is unlikely to be a problem. That said, there are reports of unpleasant incidents such as restaurants claiming to be fully booked, or shopkeepers with a suspicious eye, and travellers of north African or Arab appearance may be unlucky enough to encounter outright hostility or excessive police interest.

TELEPHONES Almost all public phones take phonecards (*télécartes*), sold at railway stations and *tabacs*. Many call boxes also accept credit cards, but coin-operated phones are rare. For calling **within Paris**, you'll always need to dial the regional code first – ☎01. Local calls are inexpensive, especially off peak, though hotel phones usually carry a significant mark-up. Domestic and international off-peak rates run at weekends and weekdays from 7pm to 8am. At peak rates, €1 gets you about five minutes to the US or Britain. The number for French directory enquiries and operator assistance is ☎12.

France operates on the European GSM **mobile phone** standard, so travellers from Britain can bring theirs from home; US cellphones, however, won't work in Paris unless they're tri-band.

TIPPING Service is almost always included in restaurant bills, so you don't need to leave more than small change. Taxi drivers and hairdressers expect around ten percent. You should tip only at the most expensive hotels; in other cases you're probably tipping the proprietor or their family.

Language

Language

Basics

Paris isn't the easiest place to learn French: many Parisians speak a hurried slang and will often reply to your carefully enunciated question in English. Despite this, it's worth making the effort, and knowing a few essentials can make all the difference. Even just saying "Bonjour monsieur/madame" and then gesticulating will usually secure you a smile and helpful service.

What follows is a run-down of essential words and phrases. For more detail, get *French: A Rough Guide Dictionary Phrase Book*, which has an extensive vocabulary, a detailed menu reader and useful dialogues.

Pronunciation

Vowels are the hardest sounds to get right. Roughly:

a	as in hat		o	as in hot
e	as in get		o/au	as in over
é	between get and gate		ou	as in food
è	between get and gut		u	as in a pursed-lip, clipped version
eu	like the u in hurt			of toot
i	as in machine			

More awkward are the combinations in/im, en/em, on/om, un/um at the end of words, or followed by consonants other than n or m Again, roughly:

in/im	like the "an" in anxious		on/om	like "on" said by some-
an/am, en/em	like "on" said with a			one with a heavy cold
nasal accent			un/um	like the "u" in under-
			stand	

Consonants are much as in English, except that ch is always sh, h is silent, th is the same as t, ll is like the y in "yes" when preceded by the letter "i", w is v, and r is growled (or rolled).

Words and phrases

Basics	
Yes	Oui
No	Non
Please	S'il vous plaît
Thank you	Merci
Excuse me	Pardon/excusez-moi
Sorry	Pardon, madame/Je m'excuse
Hello	Bonjour
Hello (phone)	Allô
Goodbye	Au revoir
Good morning/ afternoon	Bonjour
Good evening	Bonsoir
Good night	Bonne nuit
How are you?	Comment allez-vous?/Ça va?
Fine, thanks	Très bien, merci
I don't know	Je ne sais pas
Do you speak English?	Vous parlez anglais?
How do you say …in French?	Comment ça se dit…en français?

What's your name?	Comment vous appelez-vous?
My name is …	Je m'appelle …
I'm English/ Irish/ Scottish/ Welsh/ American/	Je suis anglais(e)/ irlandais(e)/ écossais(e)/ gallois(e)/ américain(e)/
OK/agreed	D'accord
I understand	Je comprends
I don't understand	Je ne comprends pas
Can you speak slower?	S'il vous plaît, parlez moins vite
Today	Aujourd'hui
Yesterday	Hier
Tomorrow	Demain
In the morning	Le matin
In the afternoon	L'après-midi
In the evening	Le soir
Now	Maintenant
Later	Plus tard
Here	Ici
There	Là
This one	Ceci
That one	Cela
Open	Ouvert
Closed	Fermé
Big	Grand
Small	Petit
More	Plus
Less	Moins
A little	Un peu
A lot	Beaucoup
Half	La moitié
Inexpensive	Bon marché/Pas cher
Expensive	Cher
Good	Bon
Bad	Mauvais
Hot	Chaud
Cold	Froid
With	Avec
Without	Sans

Questions

Where?	Où?
How?	Comment?
How many	Combien?
How much is it?	C'est combien?
When?	Quand?
Why?	Pourquoi?
At what time?	À quelle heure?
What is/Which is?	Quel est?

Getting around

Which way is it to the Eiffel Tower?	S'il vous plaît, pour aller à la Tour Eiffel?
Where is the nearest Métro?	Où est le Métro le plus proiche?
Bus	Bus
Bus stop	Arrêt
Train	Train
Boat	Bâteau
Plane	Avion
Railway station	Gare
Platform	Quai
What time does it leave?	Il part à quelle heure?
What time does it arrive?	Il arrive à quelle heure?
A ticket to …	Un billet pour …
Single ticket	Aller simple
Return ticket	Aller retour
Where are you going?	Vous allez où?
I'm going to …	Je vais à …
I want to get off at …	Je voudrais descendre à …
Near	Près/pas loin
Far	Loin
Left	À gauche
Right	À droite

Accommodation

A room for one /two people	Une chambre pour une/deux personnes
With a double bed	Avec un grand lit
A room with a shower	Une chambre avec douche
A room with a bath	Une chambre avec salle de bains
For one/two/ three nights	Pour une/deux/trois nuit(s)
With a view	Avec vue
Key	Clef
To iron	Repasser
Do laundry	Faire la lessive
Sheets	Draps
Blankets	Couvertures
Quiet	Calme
Noisy	Bruyant
Hot water	Eau chaude
Cold water	Eau froide
Is breakfast included?	Est-ce que le petit déjeuner est compris?

I would like breakfast	Je voudrais prendre le petit déjeuner
I don't want breakfast	Je ne veux pas le petit déjeuner
Youth hostel	Auberge de jeunesse

Eating out

I'd like to reserve	Je voudrais réserver
...a table	...une table
...for two people,	...pour deux personnes
at eight thirty	à vingt heures et demie
I'm having the €15 menu	Je prendrai le menu à quinze euros
Waiter!	Monsieur/madame! (never "garçon")
The bill, please	l'addition, s'il vous plaît

Days

Monday	Lundi
Tuesday	Mardi
Wednesday	Mercredi
Thursday	Jeudi
Friday	Vendredi
Saturday	Samedi
Sunday	Dimanche

Numbers

1	un
2	deux
3	trois
4	quatre
5	cinq
6	six
7	sept
8	huit
9	neuf
10	dix
11	onze
12	douze
13	treize
14	quatorze
15	quinze
16	seize
17	dix-sept
18	dix-huit
19	dix-neuf
20	vingt
21	vingt-et-un
22	vingt-deux
30	trente
40	quarante
50	cinquante
60	soixante
70	soixante-dix
75	soixante-quinze
80	quatre-vingts
90	quatre-vingt-dix
95	quatre-vingt-quinze
100	cent
101	cent un
200	deux cents
1000	mille
2000	deux mille
1,000,000	un million

Menu reader

Essentials

déjeuner	lunch
dîner	dinner
menu	set menu
à la carte	individually priced dishes
entrées	starters
les plats	main courses
pain	bread
beurre	butter
fromage	cheese
oeufs	eggs
lait	milk
poivre	pepper
sel	salt
sucre	sugar
fourchette	fork
couteau	knife
cuillère	spoon
bio	organic
à la vapeur	steamed
au four	baked
cru	raw
frit	fried
fumé	smoked
grillé	grilled
rôti	roast
salé	salted/savoury
sucré	sweet
à emporter	takeaway

Drinks

eau minérale	mineral water
eau gazeuse	fizzy water

eau plate	still water
carte des vins	wine list
une pression	a glass of beer
un café	coffee (espresso)
un crème	white coffee
bouteille	bottle
verre	glass
un quart/demi de rouge/blanc	a quarter/half-litre of red/white house wine
Un (verre de) rouge/blanc	a glass of white/red wine

Snacks

crêpe	pancake (sweet)
un sandwich /une baguette	sandwich
croque -monsieur	grilled cheese & ham sandwich
panini	flat toasted italian sandwich
omelette	omelette
nature	plain
aux fines herbes	with herbs
au fromage	with cheese
assiette anglaise	plate of cold meats
crudités	raw vegetables with dressings

Fish (poisson) and seafood (fruits de mer)

anchois	anchovies
brème	bream
brochet	pike
cabillaud	cod
carrelet	plaice
colin	hake
coquilles st-jacques	scallops
crabe	crab
crevettes	shrimps/prawns
daurade	sea bream
flétan	halibut
friture	whitebait
hareng	herring
homard	lobster
huîtres	oysters
langoustines	crayfish (scampi)
limande	lemon sole
lotte de mer	monkfish
loup de mer	sea bass
maquereau	mackerel
merlan	whiting
morue	dried, salted cod

moules (marinière)	mussels (with shallots in white wine sauce)
raie	skate
rouget	red mullet
saumon	salmon
sole	sole
thon	tuna
truite	trout
turbot	turbot

Meat (viande) and poultry (volaille)

agneau	lamb
andouillette	tripe sausage
bavette	beef flank steak
bœuf	beef
bifteck	steak
boudin noir	black pudding
caille	quail
canard	duck
contrefilet	sirloin roast
dinde	turkey
entrecôte	ribsteak
faux filet	sirloin steak
foie	liver
foie gras	fattened (duck/goose) liver
gigot (d'agneau)	leg (of lamb)
grillade	grilled meat
hachis	chopped meat or mince hamburger
jambon	ham
lapin, lapereau	rabbit, young rabbit
lard, lardons	bacon, diced bacon
merguez	spicy, red sausage
oie	goose
onglet	cut of beef
porc	pork
poulet	chicken
poussin	baby chicken
rognons	kidneys
tête de veau	calf's head (in jelly)
veau	veal
venaison	venison

Steaks

bleu	almost raw
saignant	rare
à point	medium
bien cuit	well done

Garnishes and sauces

beurre blanc	sauce of white wine & shallots, with butter

chasseur	white wine, mushrooms & shallots
forestière	with bacon & mushroom
fricassée	rich, creamy sauce
mornay	cheese sauce
pays d'auge	cream & cider
piquante	gherkins or capers, vinegar & shallots
provençale	tomatoes, garlic, olive oil & herbs

Vegetables (légumes), herbs (herbes) and spices (épices)

ail	garlic
artichaut	artichoke
asperges	asparagus
basilic	basil
betterave	beetroot
carotte	carrot
céleri	celery
champignons	mushrooms
chou (rouge)	(red) cabbage
chou-fleur	cauliflower
concombre	cucumber
cornichon	gherkin
échalotes	shallots
endive	chicory
épinards	spinach
estragon	tarragon
fenouil	fennel
flageolets	white beans
gingembre	ginger
haricots	beans
verts	string (french)
rouges	kidney
beurres	butter
lentilles	lentils
maïs	corn (maize)
moutarde	mustard
oignon	onion
pâtes	pasta
persil	parsley
petits pois	peas
pois chiche	chickpeas
poireau	leek
poivron	sweet pepper
(vert, rouge)	(green, red)
pommes	potatoes
(de terre)	
primeurs	spring vegetables
riz	rice
safran	saffron
salade verte	green salad
tomate	tomato
truffes	truffles

Fruits (fruits) and nuts (noix)

abricot	apricot
amandes	almonds
ananas	pineapple
banane	banana
brugnon, nectarine	nectarine
cacahouète	peanut
cassis	blackcurrants
cerises	cherries
citron	lemon
citron vert	lime
figues	figs
fraises	strawberries
framboises	raspberries
groseilles	redcurrants & gooseberries
mangue	mango
marrons	chestnuts
melon	melon
noisette	hazelnut
noix	nuts
orange	orange
pamplemousse	grapefruit
pêche	peach
pistache	pistachio
poire	pear
pomme	apple
prune	plum
pruneau	prune
raisins	grapes

Desserts (desserts or entremets) and pastries (pâtisserie)

bavarois	refers to the mould, could be mousse or custard
brioche	sweet, high yeast breakfast roll
coupe	a serving of ice cream
crème chantilly	vanilla-flavoured & sweetened whipped cream
crème fraîche	sour cream
crème pâtissière	thick eggy pastry-filling
fromage blanc	cream cheese
glace	ice cream
parfait	frozen mousse, sometimes ice cream
petits fours	bite-sized cakes/pastries
tarte	tart
yaourt, yogourt	yoghurt

Index and small print

INDEX

A Rough Guide to Rough Guides

Paris DIRECTIONS is published by Rough Guides. The first *Rough Guide to Greece*, published in 1982, was a student scheme that became a publishing phenomenon. The immediate success of the book – with numerous reprints and a Thomas Cook prize shortlisting – spawned a series that rapidly covered dozens of destinations. Rough Guides had a ready market among low-budget backpackers, but soon also acquired a much broader and older readership that relished Rough Guides' wit and inquisitiveness as much as their enthusiastic, critical approach. Everyone wants value for money, but not at any price. Rough Guides soon began supplementing the "rougher" information about hostels and low-budget listings with the kind of detail on restaurants and quality hotels that independent-minded visitors on any budget might expect, whether on business in New York or trekking in Thailand. These days the guides offer recommendations from shoestring to luxury and a large number of destinations around the globe, including almost every country in the Americas and Europe, more than half of Africa and most of Asia and Australasia. Rough Guides now publish:

- Travel guides to more than 200 worldwide destinations
- Dictionary phrasebooks to 22 major languages
- Maps printed on rip-proof and waterproof Polyart™ paper
- Music guides running the gamut from Opera to Elvis
- Reference books on topics as diverse as the Weather and Shakespeare
- World Music CDs in association with World Music Network

Visit **www.roughguides.com** to see our latest publications.

Publishing Information

This 1st edition published May 2004 by **Rough Guides Ltd**, 80 Strand, London WC2R 0RL. 345 Hudson St, 4th Floor, New York, NY 10014, USA.

Distributed by the Penguin Group
Penguin Books Ltd, 80 Strand, London WC2R 0RL
Penguin Group (USA), 375 Hudson Street, NY 10014, USA
Penguin Group (Australia), 487 Maroondah Highway, PO Box 257, Ringwood, Victoria 3134, Australia
Penguin Group (Canada), 10 Alcorn Avenue, Toronto, Ontario, Canada M4V 1E4
Penguin Group (NZ), 182–190 Wairau Road, Auckland 10, New Zealand
Typeset in Bembo and Helvetica to an original design by Henry Iles.
Printed and bound in Italy by Graphicom

© Rough Guides May 2004

224pp includes index
A catalogue record for this book is available from the British Library

ISBN 1-84353-317-0

The publishers and authors have done their best to ensure the accuracy and currency of all the information in **Paris DIRECTIONS**, however, they can accept no responsibility for any loss, injury, or inconvenience sustained by any traveller as a result of information or advice contained in the guide.

1   3   5   7   9   8   6   4   2

Help us update

We've gone to a lot of effort to ensure that the first edition of **Paris DIRECTIONS** is accurate and up-to-date. However, things change – places get "discovered", opening hours are notoriously fickle, restaurants and rooms raise prices or lower standards. If you feel we've got it wrong or left something out, we'd like to know, and if you can remember the address, the price, the time, the phone number, so much the better.

We'll credit all contributions, and send a copy of the next edition (or any other DIRECTIONS guide or Rough Guide if you prefer) for the best letters. Everyone who writes to us and isn't already a subscriber will receive a copy of our full-colour thrice-yearly newsletter. Please mark letters: **"Paris DIRECTIONS Update"** and send to: Rough Guides, 80 Strand, London WC2R 0RL, or Rough Guides, 4th Floor, 345 Hudson St, New York, NY 10014. Or send an email to **mail@roughguides.com**

Have your questions answered and tell others about your trip at **www.roughguides.atinfopop.com**

The authors

Ruth Blackmore is a Senior Editor at Rough Guides in London. She is the co-author of the *Rough Guide to Paris* and a contributor to the *Rough Guide to France* and the *Rough Guide to Classical Music*.

James McConnachie is a writer and photographer based in London. He is the author of the *Rough Guide to the Loire* and co-author of the Rough Guides to Paris and Nepal. He has also contributed to the Rough Guides to France, Spain, Italy, Venice and Florence.

Acknowledgements

Ruth would especially like to thank Fenella for help with research; James, Carole and Loic; and Dylan for his advice and support.

James would like to say a special thank you to Eva, Guillaume and Marjorie for their advice and companionship in Paris, and to Alice for all her support. Thanks too to Pierre Loechner for his musical expertise.

The authors would like to thank Eva Loechner for her thorough and timely work in fact-checking the guide, as well as Martin Dunford, Geoff Howard, Diana Jarvis, Sharon Martins, Mark Thomas and Andy Turner at Rough Guides. In Paris, thanks to Sandrine Adass, Musée d'Art et d'Histoire du Judaïsme; Catherine Adam, Musée Delacroix; Stephanie Barral, Alain Ducasse; Mme Barthélemy, Barthélemy; M Bergcot, Musée de l'Armée; Valery Boucher, Hédiard; Mme Boulinier, Grande Galerie d'Evolution; Lionel Bordeaux, Mairie de Paris; Philippe Bourgeois; Georges Brunel, Musée Cognacq-Jay; Candilhe Calcaltagirone, Café Georges; Brigitte Camus; Madame Canipel, Hôtel Ermitage; Mlle Celine, Rex Club; Jean-Pierre Chauvet, Musée Picasso; Catherine Decaure, Musée Carnavalet; Stephanie Delaserve, Musée du Vin; Mlle Delfine, Zadig & Voltaire; Sylvester Engbrox, Musée Rodin; Claire Fine, Disney; Yves Gagneux, Musée Balzac; Stephanie Froger, Musée de l'Armée; Mlle Gallais, Musée de l'Armée; Xavier Héraud, Têtu; Juliette Laffon, Musée Bourdelle; Florence Lannuzel, Musée Rodin; Helene Lefevre, Musée Guimet; M Louis, Lasserre; Jerome Manoukian, Musée Rodin; Mme Marie Odile, Hôtel du Globe; Mme Maurer, Musée Moreau; Niko Melissano, Musée du Louvre; Mme Messina, Site de Création Contemporaine; M Monnin, Hôtel Pavillon de la Reine; Mme Moreau, Musée Niscim-Caïmondo; Anne de Necic, Musée Galicra; Mme Nocl, Le Limonaire; Fasia Ouagurmouni, Musée Zadkine; M Papin, La Gare; Véronique Petit-Jean, Musée du Louvre; M Philippe, Square Trousseau; M Pierre, L'Ambroisie; Caroline Pons, Flo group; M Provensal, Cité de la Musique; M Reix, Le Jules Verne; Béatrice Ruggieri, L'Hôtel, Ann Samuel, Musée Carnavalet; Mme Sigal, Musée d'Art et d'Histoire du Judaïsme; Mathieu Tordjaman, Les Bains; Anne Veron, Musée d'Orsay; Bruno de Ville d'Avray, Les Egouts de Paris.

INDEX

Index

A

B

C